BIO-SPIRITUALITY

Focusing as a way to grow

by Peter A. Campbell, Ph.D.
&
Edwin M. McMahon, Ph.D.

A Campion Book

Loyola University Press
Chicago 60657

©1985 Peter A. Campbell
and Edwin M. McMahon

Loyola University Press
3441 North Ashland Avenue
Chicago, Illinois 60657

Design by J. L. Boden

Biblical quotations from the Revised Standard Version taken from *The Holy Bible and Apocrypha,* used with permission of the National Council of the Churches of Christ, New York, NY, cited as RSV.

Biblical quotations from *The New English Bible* used with permission of the publisher, Oxford University Press, 1970, cited as NEB.

Library of Congress Cataloging in Publication Data

Campbell, Peter A.
  Bio-spirituality : focusing as a way to grow.

  1. Spiritual life.   I. McMahon, Edwin M., 1930-
II. Title.
BL624.C34 1985   291.4'3   84-21328
ISBN 0-8294-0478-3

Contents

Foreword

Changes in therapy and human experience raise questions for faith and theology. One such development is noted in Alexander Lowen's *Bioenergetics:* "The failure of verbal therapies to produce significant changes in personality," he writes, "is responsible for an increasing interest in non-verbal and body approaches." (p. 120) In this book, Campbell and McMahon argue persuasively that a similar shift of attention to the body's wisdom is needed today for Christian spirituality. Religion of the head has left us divided from one another and from ourselves. We need to get to deeper roots of the Spirit than formulated beliefs.

The authors have found Focusing, the therapeutic method developed by Eugene Gendlin of the University of Chicago, to be a way into the body's wisdom. At one level, focusing is a therapy that helps people resolve human conflicts and get in touch with their own inner direction. At a deeper level, which is the very core of this book, focusing becomes a form of spiritual meditation that helps people find their own form of self-transcendence.

Meditation has taken many forms in world religions: from wordless, imageless centering of Zen Buddhism and Christian Zen, the mystical mantras of the Orient and the popular "Jesus Prayer" which developed within Eastern Orthodox Christianity, to the mandalas of Tibet, the icons of Orthodoxy, and the Ignatian contemplations on the mysteries of Jesus' life in Western Christianity. Each form draws a person to a transcendent cosmic truth beyond ordinary life while yet within it. Focusing has many similarities. It is a discipline of attending to the bodily "felt-sense" of what is at work in one's life. This felt-sense is more basic than words or images. However, when it touches the transcendent ground of our ongoing life, it yields fresh images and words that release life and energy formerly stifled by traditional consciousness. Thus focusing, like traditional meditation, touches a deeper cosmic process, but it does so in a way that is unique to each individual in his or her own time and place. We each share this "cosmic process"—which the authors relate to the divine Spirit in the world—so that it can heal our isolation and fear and lead us to recognize our participation in a dynamic universal truth. If many were growing in this spiritual focusing, God's image would emerge ever more clearly in our world.

The process of focusing, seen at that spiritual depth, gives the authors a fresh way of viewing Christian truth as well as the truth of other worldviews. Since one's felt-sense is prior to specific beliefs or formulations, focusing promises to unite persons of various persuasions, to heal wounds of misunderstanding and alienation, and to open people to sharing a common future unfolding in the world. It touches into a level of humanity united in a single evolving world, a "gifted" or "graced" unity that is not caused by ego efforts but rather by surrender to this common underlying process.

Yet we resist this unity for many reasons. Our ego structures, both individual and communal, often mask weakness and pain. Focusing makes one attend to areas of hurt and weakness lodged deep in the memories of the body, which forgets nothing. Conventional beliefs and orthodoxies often merely protect us from these vulnerable areas. We fight and make war to defend these beliefs, and it is a veritable "crucifixion" to face the insecurity of surrendering them. But further, our ego structures are "moral achievements." They discipline unbridled sexuality and aggression that our Western Christian culture sees lurking in our bodies. Our permissive generation is in reaction against such Victorian mores, but the same separation of body from spirit lies in both. Sexuality is alienated from responsible spirituality. The body's desires then get separated from their deeper awareness of "being unto death," and their deeper ground in God. As Ernest Becker pointed out in *The Denial of Death,* we flee death and escape into idealizations of sexual conquest and success. But the body knows the dying within, and only by facing it can we face our true reality and our true spirituality. Focusing thus contacts our inner vulnerability and repressed pain, but that very contact releases new energy and fresh hope.

The courageous decision to face that inner truth is how Campbell and McMahon understand conversion and faith. That faith is grounded not in formulated beliefs but in the experience of the unfolding process itself. The very process of believing gives us an analogous way of understanding its deepest ground, the triune God. "I" focus on a "felt-sense" which "unfolds" into who I am in the process of becoming. Analogously, the Father (I) forms his perfect Image (felt-sense) which gives rise to an unfolding process of integration and self-transcendence (Holy Spirit). Focusing is a doorway beyond formulations of belief to faith or believing itself. As one moves more deeply into it, every event, every "felt-meaning," can become a religious event opening one to incarnate Spirit unfolding in evolution. Focusing does not *cause* this redemptive contact with Spirit. It opens the way. The transforming event itself is always perceived as gift—as grace—and a growing gratitude and reverence emerge in one who lives out this spiritual type of focusing.

The perspectives opened by spiritual focusing are exciting. Yet several questions will likely come to the Christian's mind that will need to be addressed before he or she can be fully receptive to this new view. For the Christian, Jesus is the unique mediator of relationship to the Father. How does his person appear as one opens to the cosmic process? Should not Christian meditation center on Jesus? Similarly, Jesus is the Second Person of the Trinity, not just an expression of the self-knowledge of the Father. And the Holy Spirit is "another Paraclete" (*John 14:16*), another person in the triune God, not just a process of spiritual evolution. How do these personal characteristics appear in the focusing process? Further, do we not believe in doctrinal definitions that remain permanently true, such as the Son is of "like being" with the Father (Nicaea) and fully human (Chalcedon)? Are these truths preserved if one takes one's ground at a preverbal level? Or more specifically, can we fully trust our bodily wisdom when we have experienced how narrow desires or angers have led us away from God and others? How is one to discern between movements that are of God and those that are not? Surely not everything that transcends ordinary consciousness is of God.

These are serious questions that will need to be faced. Yet they do not have to be fully resolved before one enters fully into the process of spiritual focusing so well presented in this book. Focusing as a spiritual discipline has been a help to many who no doubt interpret their experience according to their own frame of reference. The theoretical questions do not have to be fully resolved before the reader can profit from the method of meditation presented here.

For Christians who want to pursue the theoretical questions more fully, the following observations may be of help. A first observation regards theological method. Every theologian or reflective Christian frames questions and understands according to his or her religious experience or conversion. An academician asks academic questions, a mystic mystical questions. The authors show that our bodies and their memories are key to authentic experience. Since how one interprets Scripture or tradition, God or Trinity, depends on what experience one appeals to as analogous, we will have to get beyond concepts to the underlying bodily experience if our interpretation is to be authentic. Focusing is an excellent way to this bodily experience.

This means, secondly, that the body is far more important than Western theology or spirituality has conceded. The negative attitude of Western Christianity toward the body is not biblical. The authors of Scripture saw the human person as embodied. It was the Greeks and the Fathers influenced by Greek philosophy who distinguished between body and spirit in a way that contributed to our modern separation of body and spirit. The evangelists believed in the resurrection of *body,* not just the immortality of the soul (a Greek notion), and they came to see this resurrection as already active in believers. That means that our bodily existence is already being transformed through the Spirit of Jesus' resurrection, and that the believer can touch this Spirit at the depth of inner experience and in the bond of love uniting believers.

Thirdly, however, a caution is needed. Is there such a thing as noninterpreted experience? Or is the interpretation or symbol that arises spontaneously from one's unconscious a final criterion of meaning? It seems already to be a theological option to believe in a universal unity of cosmic process grounding bodily awareness. One may believe, as Jung seems to have done following Kant, that one's experience of God is uniquely individual, and that a "common unity" would only reduce people to a low common denominator. Or regarding death, the body may, as the authors suggest, have intimations of existence beyond death, or it may lead others of a more existentialist bent to see death as a barrier to be faced with Stoic heroism.

Does bodily experience move one decisively to either option? Is it not rather a prior faith or conversion that moves one to interpret bodily experience in one or the other way? What the authors present seems already to be based on a Christian option for universal salvation or an oriental view of the unity of all being. The basis of that option is not simply bodily awareness of spirit, as important as that may be. As Christians, the authors believe in the resurrected Lordship of Jesus and the Spirit as potentially universal. The Zen Buddhist or Hindu Advaitist believes in the nonduality of all experience as revealed through enlightenment. These basic conversions color each one's bodily awareness as well as being affected by that awareness. Ultimately everyone uses some norm to interpret experience, and experience in turn affects the understanding of the norm.

Finally, for the Christian that norm is the person and life-death-resurrection of Jesus Christ. What effect would this specifically Christian perspective have on spiritual focusing? What importance does focusing then have? It would seem to be a very significant way of becoming aware of one's unique embodied being in the here and now in dialogue with the normative Spirit of Jesus' life. The Spiritual Exercises of St. Ignatius lead the exercitant into contemplations of the mysteries of Jesus' life, death, and resurrection and ask the person to "draw fruit," that is, to bring the Spirit of Jesus' life into dialogue with one's own life. Focusing seems ideally suited to complement such a process, that is, to bring the uniqueness of one's own spiritual process into dialogue with Jesus' life. One's felt-sense gives rise to an image or word which releases a shift of perspective or energy. For the Christian, the deepest meaning of this shift is that it transforms believers into the image of God revealed in the Spirit of Jesus' life. Thus, if one related one's experience to the scriptural portrait of Jesus, one would not only gain new insight into Jesus' life, but also illumine and energize one's own life in a new way.

Without saying it, the authors have used a similar method of correlation by using Judaeo-Christian Scripture to help illumine focusing, and by using focusing to open new meanings of Scripture. All I would add is the interpersonal dimension—the dialogue with the person and life of Jesus and the persons of the Trinity which is at the heart of Christian spirituality. Other religious traditions would find other meanings, but openness to experience as basic to dialogue would lead each tradition to respect the process of the others and thus lead to a pluralistic unity analogous to the cosmic unity envisioned in the book. Spiritual focusing would thus open each of us to the excitement of seeing our lives unfold in a common spirit, which the Christian would see as rooted in the one Spirit of Jesus who also reveals the Father's love. Focusing does not interpret itself, but it may well be an important key to unlock the mysteries of God's work in the depth of creation and in each individual, revealed in Jesus' life and Spirit and ever unfolding in human evolution.

Robert T. Sears, S.J.
Loyola University of Chicago

Preface

Many years ago, Carl Jung noted something that continues to intrigue us. Writing of Western society's desperate need for a more integral spiritual discipline he made the following observation:

> No insight is gained . . . by imitating methods which have grown up under totally different psychological conditions. In the course of the centuries the West will produce its own yoga and it will be on the basis laid down by Christianity.[1]

We have often wondered whether such an event might occur within our lifetime. Would we be fortunate enough to experience an emerging Western "yoga," some integral expression of our own culture and spirit that might lead us home to ourselves?

Throughout the past decade, bits and pieces of a potential orientation have gradually fallen into place for us. All the data, obviously, has not yet come in. Much emerges not from religious sources but from the human sciences. It is there that our Western appreciation of bodily felt awareness has been prized more than anywhere else.

At the same time, we have found buried within the Judaeo-Christian tradition some neglected and little used information that may well unlock the secret of consciousness evolution. In this book we plan to describe certain teachings from this ancient heritage which contain clues about the nature of consciousness and its evolution. These clues are equally applicable to non-Christians as well as to Christians *when they can be approached out of a bodily-felt perspective.* That perceptual shift makes all the difference. It opens a refreshing new direction for anyone interested in spirituality.

The approach to bodily awareness which we describe in the following pages is called "Focusing." It was originated by Dr. Eugene Gendlin at the University of Chicago. Part of our book describes the practical details of how we teach Focusing. But our main point is to demonstrate that what began as a purely therapeutic tool has the potential to become a widespread and accessible spiritual path for ordinary people during the 1980s and beyond.

We have sought to avoid the denominational and dogmatic in what you are about to read. Our work responds to an invitation which Dr. James Fadiman, then president of the Association for Transpersonal Psychology, made several years ago. He asked us to find within the Judaeo-Christian tradition clues that might support Transpersonal Psychology's effort to enlarge and understand the human person and the growth process.

Putting all this together, we have tried in what follows to reach out toward those whom Abraham Maslow has described as "Serious Seekers." Denominational affiliation or lack thereof is not the primary issue. Rather, we address the quest for a psychologically sound, practical approach to an embodied spirituality. One that acknowledges a deeper *felt sense* for ultimate meaning.

The purpose of this book, which has taken twelve years of research, writing, and personal experience to complete, is to make some contribution toward developing a new paradigm for Western spirituality. Not a paradigm of all-encompassing theoretical synthesis, but a transformed way of being in and experiencing ourselves.

There is mystery within bodily knowing. Metamorphosis occurs when we can be faithful to the depth of ourselves. This book is about the journey toward such faithfulness, and about the body of felt experiencing within which it occurs.

Introduction

"A lookout point in the universe"

The year was 1799. A French soldier attached to an expeditionary force in Egypt was busy preparing fortifications for the Nile Delta town of Rashid—called Rosetta by the Europeans. Suddenly, during the course of his excavation he unearthed a slab from an ancient temple. It was made of black basalt, stood about a meter high, and contained what appeared to be the same inscription written in three different languages—Egyptian hieroglyphics, Demotic, and Greek.

Up to this point in time Egyptian hieroglyphics had remained indecipherable. They had resisted every attempt to crack the coded language which veiled hidden wonders within this most ancient civilization. Now, with the chance thrusting of a laborer's shovel the inscrutable barrier had been broken. By comparing the Greek letters for Ptolemy and Cleopatra with their hieroglyphic counterparts, a door was finally opened. The first ray of light in modern times fell across the dark interior of this long-silent culture. Scholars hovered in awe before the treasure which now lay at their fingertips. The Rosetta Stone was their key. It was a lookout point from which to peer into the soul of a vast, unspoken civilization.

The inward journey outlined in this book may be compared to the first steps in a venture that can lead not merely into the mysteries of another culture; it can be an opening forward as the human species prepares for the next phase of consciousness evolution itself!

Yet, there are still more parallels in this journey with the finding of the Rosetta Stone. There are significant clues about what lies ahead within human unfolding. A superb humanistic vision can light our way on this journey into ourselves. Much of the revelation about what it means to be human, however, lies coded within the wisdom tradition of world religions. There is a silent treasure there hidden beneath centuries of neglect and misinterpretation.

This book grew from searching, searching for a practical way to enter ordinary living so the meaning of being human and being uniquely oneself might lead each of us forward into the mystery of some larger Awareness. These pages will attempt to describe the ingredients of a lived spirituality which actually facilitates change. We are not concerned with change in the realm of religious *ideas*. Rather, we look toward a transformation which will support human wholeness as this can unfold within a greater organismic evolution—a growing cosmic congruence.

This is not, therefore, a collection of denominational religious teachings or truths. We describe, instead, a quality of human consciousness, a lifestyle wherein an awareness potential of *the body* is absolutely indispensable for spiritual knowing. We call this capacity for more integral presence *bio-spirituality*.

Once our entire consciousness is encouraged to open and mature, then the root of our biological connectedness to some vast Process of Unification can gradually reveal itself within our daily lives. There is an awareness within our bodies that leads beyond ourselves. A bio-consciousness. Bio-presence. It does not confine us to what we can figure out and control with our minds, but it turns, instead, toward *an openness* within bodily knowing.

Whether we choose to recognize it or not, each of us is an integral living cell within the evolution of some Larger Body Process. The maturation of this awareness, however, does not occur by reason of what we *do*, but by virtue of a wholeness we *allow* to break through inside our selves. Unity within the human family, our planet, and some greater cosmic congruence matures inside the knowing that is proper to our bodies. It is not so much thinking as *resonance*. The tuning fork of evolution strikes an inviting chord within the organicity of ourselves.

In the pages which follow we would like to share the beginnings of a bio-spiritual treasure hunt. It is a journey which has drawn the two of us into a dramatic new perspective on the mysteries and revelation contained within our own religious tradition. Certain clues within the Judaeo-Christian heritage have opened for us a challenging new way to look at the bio-spiritual implications of *human development itself!*

We believe a time has come in human history, if for no other reason than for the survival of life on our planet, when we must turn our energy and our priorities toward encouraging just such consciousness-potential. We need to find simple, practical ways to support this humanizing capability within millions of people so that an experience of planetary unity may be revealed.

People blocked from growth cannot assimilate the crucial, life-saving data that lies hidden beneath their narrow and limited perception. When personal meaning becomes unblocked, however, they can often be freed from the fear and defensiveness which so often lead to violence.

In this book we want to share with you, our reader, a mode of self-awareness which offers an exciting and significant step toward developing a bio-spirituality that responds to these critical needs. We describe what we feel are the key ingredients in a humanizing spirituality. These include psychological dynamics which transcend the teachings of any particular religion. Yet they are found in the wisdom literature and perennial philosophy of the world's great spiritual traditions. They are often arcane, enigmatic, and inaccessible to the average person; popular religion has rarely been able to utilize the wisdom that lies hidden within the venerable patrimonies of the past.

The religious experience of unity and wholeness lies rooted in a bio-spirituality deep within the evolution of ourselves and of the cosmos itself. The religions of the world must now step toward this energizing experience on a massive popular scale if they are to make a significant contribution to the course of human history. Values, perceptions, and lifestyles must change radically or the world's growing arsenal of nuclear weapons will eventually destroy us.

Religion seems to be at a crossroads in our time. Because of an exhausting preoccupation with morality, it has generally failed to call forth any depth of spiritual vision within its adherents. "Doing good and avoiding evil" simply does not provide the energetic stuff from which an evolutionary vision can be fashioned. Without breadth, height, and depth—the fresh air of mountain tops—religion tends to be small and niggardly. There is an inevitable decline.

The priest/scientist Pierre Teilhard de Chardin expressed the problem well:

> In its present state Morality offers a painful spectacle of confusion. Apart from a few elementary laws of individual justice, empirically established and blindly followed, who can say what is good and what is evil? Can we even maintain that Good and Evil exist while the evolutionary course on which we are embarked has no clear direction? Is striving really a better thing than enjoyment, disinterest better than

self-interest, kindness better than compulsion?
Lacking a look-out point in the Universe, the most
sharply opposed doctrines on these vital matters can
be plausibly defended.[1]

"A look-out point in the universe." That's what we
want to share in this book. Not some new doctrine or
interpretation, but a way to stand in ourselves. A quality
of experience. A point of spiritual resonance.

When Teilhard de Chardin wrote his reflections on
morality in 1942, he lamented that the best way of reaching the desired lookout point had yet to be found. In this
book we want to describe what we regard as an important
step toward such a perspective.

The practical details of this step have been worked
out in their initial stages by Dr. Eugene T. Gendlin.

Through therapeutic research, he and his colleagues
have indirectly opened an extraordinary doorway into the
realm of spiritual awareness. His pioneering effort called
Focusing[2] is a simple way of attending to meaning that is
felt in the body.

We believe that the regular use of Focusing can support significant movement toward a humane valuing
process. This is valuing which is not drawn from the
mind's distinction between right and wrong but from a
deeper sense for direction, purpose, and context within
the cosmos. There is support within our bodies for unitary
consciousness. Focusing, we believe, can contribute to a
spirituality that nourishes cosmic congruence irrespec-
tive of a person's religious affiliation.

Without some practical "look-out point in the universe," world religions and all people who espouse unitive teachings face an indescribably bleak alternative.
Unless we can find a way to live these noble teachings,
unless we take concrete steps *to put our bodies where our
good intentions are,* unless we discover some path through
the barrier of impotence which so impedes progress in
religion today, we risk falling victim to the growing tech-

nology of planetary destruction. Focusing touches the feelings of fear, frustration, and lack of presence which nourish the suspicions, mistrust, and hatreds that inevitably lead toward war.

The way ahead, of course, lies within ourselves. But discovering the lookout point means learning *to be* in each day, in each passing moment according to the truth and actuality of its *connectedness*. To find this spiritual dimension within ourselves we must first know the truth of how we really *feel* about things, people, and events. We must touch those deeper meanings that our bodies express.

There is a *felt* truth, a *felt* meaning, a *felt* direction within each of us, an embodied sense that can free us and guide us into the future. In-touch living *connects!* It allows values and behavior to change. This is what we mean by bio-spirituality.

Both of us find that Focusing helps us reach this inner knowing. It enables us to sort out our experiences when things are not *right* at a deeper level than that which our intellects can perceive. When reason can only guess at the cause — and not always accurately — our body's awareness of meaning can offer us a direction for change from inside. *Thinking* so often gets in the way of those felt shifts wherein the real cause of alienation, destructive behavior, pain, and confusion can begin to dissipate.

The religions and spiritual movements of the world must step beyond doctrines into this realm of bodily experience, risky though it may seem. What lies ahead will transform old identities and unseat many sacred idols. It will overturn what had formerly been touched only by risking the wrath of the gods.

But if this step can be taken, we believe it will mark the beginning of a new age in human believing. A believing born of change! Discovering a lookout point in the universe may quite literally "renew the face of the earth." The world's religions might even become less competitive, less aggressive, less a source of division between individuals and a block to global wholeness.

The decision making of nations is always a human process. When people begin to touch the deeper unity that can be sensed in their bodies, they will be less likely to choose the path of nuclear destruction. Beyond the darkness of egoism lies an innate sociability and goodness which, through Focusing, can break through to the light of day. To the extent that more and more people break *through* the blockages which hinder the unfolding of their own unique life-meaning, to that extent they will discover a personal freedom and *choice* when they confront the issue of nuclear proliferation. People out of touch with themselves have no real alternative than to constantly prepare for war. Anyone in conflict with himself or herself must inevitably view the world in exactly the same manner. Inner tensions, conflicts and struggles are projected outward into the life of our planet. Multiplied over and over, the momentum of massive inner frustration becomes, finally, in our time the horror of possible nuclear holocaust.

Focusing can address this critical issue of thwarted human meaning. It unveils an inner spiritual resource which is compatible with the unitive teachings and goals of most world religions and philosophies.

Given such a perspective, the two of us, year by year, continue to evaluate our own religious practices, beliefs, and tradition. Much has not measured up. Much has seemed off-the-track and actually harmful to this journey. But we have also discovered something that certainly exists in other traditions as well. Woven into the patrimony of our past lie intriguing clues and revelations about what it means to be human. An exciting, profound invitation to journey farther into our humanity emerges as we continue to explore the roots of our own religious heritage.

In this book we will describe some of these invitations. They tell us far more about ourselves than they tell us about God. There is wisdom here, wisdom we all need as citizens of this planet and cosmos—no matter what our religious or nonreligious orientation.

The deeper *felt meaning* behind special words within our Christian revelation can help everyone, believer and nonbeliever alike, to uncover an inner resource, a broadened *psychological* sense for what it means to be human. There is a bigger picture within bodily knowing. Human awareness is only the opening movement within the vast symphonic arrangement which draws consciousness forward. There is a world beyond ego which transcends all of our foot-dragging resistance. There is *withinness* which uncovers a startling new identity. The roots of individual awareness are far broader than any limited canvas upon which they happen to be painted! We each say "I" out of a vast reservoir which as yet we only dimly perceive. Within the unfolding inwardness of humankind one senses a growing readiness for a momentous new birth.

Teilhard de Chardin suggested that we need some "lookout point in the universe" if we are to light our halting steps into the next phase of human evolution. Just such a Rosetta Stone now lies at hand. It is a unique quality of knowing that lies within our very bodies. It is a *felt sense* of a Larger Consciousness *that is already in place!*

There lies the key. We can never reason or think our way across the next evolutionary horizon. Rather, we must follow some deeper, organic rhythm. An inner resonance. The *felt sense* of Greater Awakening.

We reached a turning point in our own journey when we gradually realized that certain revelations and theological teachings in the Judaeo-Christian tradition appear to be aimed not at the mind's purely rational understanding of truth but at some deeper *organismic knowing* based on the *integration* of body and mind.

Theology speaks *about* God. But in order to appreciate the rich *humanistic* impact of such truths, one must draw on more experience than one can think in the mind. *Body-knowing, then, when integrated with mind-knowing becomes a Rosetta Stone with which to unlock the hidden evolutionary significance of latent bio-spiritual clues hidden within the Judaeo-Christian tradition and, no doubt, within other religious traditions as well.*

Perhaps now, more than at any other time in human history, the scientific and religious communities have reached a stage in their separate development where they can finally *cooperate* in the challenging exploration of bodily knowing. Our own humanity has at last become a rich ground for dialogue. A latent perspective waits to be born. But this next forward step requires the convergence of science and religion. In the words of Teilhard de Chardin:

> Religion and science are the two conjugated faces or phases of one and the same act of complete knowledge—the only one which can embrace the past and future of evolution so as to contemplate, measure and fulfil them.[3]

Among North American psychologists, Abraham Maslow was intrigued by the potential for spiritual development that lies within a more open and cooperative relationship between religion and science. The flame of his vision, though, was fanned by what he regarded as the sheer *organicity* of spiritual valuing within the person.

> My thesis is, in general, that new developments in psychology are forcing a profound change in our philosophy of science, a change so extensive that we may be able to accept the basic religious questions as a proper part of the jurisdiction of science, once science is broadened and redefined.

> A whole school of psychologists now believe that "spiritual values" are *in* the organism, so much a part of the well-functioning organism as to be *sine qua non* "*defining-characteristics*" of it.

> This thesis that religious experiences are natural experiences could be seen by churchmen with dismay,

as simply and only a further instance of science carving another chunk out of the side of organized religion—which, of course, it is. But it is also possible for a more perceptively religious man to greet this development with enthusiasm, when he realizes that what the mystics have said to be essential to the *individual's* religion is now receiving empirical support and no longer needs rest only on tradition, blind faith, temporal power, exhortation, etc. If this development is a secularizing of all religion, it is also a religionizing of all that is secular.[4]

The growth of a bio-spiritual perspective must draw on the wisdom of ancient religious traditions as well as on the contemporary appreciation of what it means to be human. In the following pages we will attempt a rough mapping out of several areas where a suitably broadened human science may be enriched by contributions from the Judaeo-Christian tradition.

Bodily knowing, for us, is a bridge that links the two realms of science and religion. It can be a common ground where each of these two different approaches can shed some of their limitations and discover together that "act of complete knowledge" which may ultimately fulfil them both.

What, then, are some of the clues hidden within a developing human science as well as within the Judaeo-Christian tradition, clues wherein any seeking person can find an openness in bodily knowing? Where are the points of resonance, the organismic windows through which the early dawn of a new creation may rouse the sleeping night of ego? How can such clues encourage *a bio-spiritual positioning* for the next leap forward in human evolution?

Imagine the numbing frustration which must have aggravated their research as early scholars pored over unintelligible hieroglyphics in the Egyptian language. The pictographic script before them provided little support for unravelling the richer message that it contained.

Those long-suffering men and women who labored to decipher that baffling code remained quite literally *outside* the meaning they so eagerly sought.

But with the Rosetta Stone in hand, a fog started to lift. Small bits and pieces of meaning began to emerge from the maddening riddle. First, probably, came proper names and places; these were soon followed by individual nouns and verbs, until, finally, entire sentences and paragraphs yielded their long-sought treasures. At last, the world *within* had opened up.

In a similar fashion, one finds special words within the Judaeo-Christian tradition, words meant to convey far more than meaning to the mind. Hidden within is a language whose full impact may only be realized to the extent that bodily knowing becomes part of our overall experience. It is a language designed to highlight shades of felt meaning which can arise from any person's inward depth of bodily knowing. But to discover such riches one must first embark upon a deliberate incarnation—*that perilous leap into the body which Christian spirituality is supposed to be all about!*

Yet all of us, Christian and non-Christian alike, hold back from this step beyond reason and control. There is an inner shrinking from the risks involved. It's much like our resistance to falling in a dream. Focusing draws us into a wilderness area within ourselves. It can at first appear to be a place of dark foreboding. One recalls those terrible warnings which were sometimes found on ancient mariners' maps. Beyond the outer fringes of exploration were inscribed those fearsome words: "Traveller beware—Here there be Dragons!"

At this point we experience the last stand of the ego. There is an unwillingness to let go of the identity and security which we have fashioned so laboriously through the careful exercise of reason and control. But unless the seed falls into the ground and dies, there can be no new life. The religious traditions of the world speak to this tension between the satisfactions of limited identity and some farther evolutionary horizon toward which our humanness seems to be called.

For many years now, we have sought to identify the elements which are essential for a bio-spirituality. It is important to realize that we have not been seeking gimmicks or techniques of transformation. Rather we want to understand how the opening of broader bio-spiritual horizons can spontaneously occur as a gratifying component within human development itself. We want to shed light upon a gifted inner ecology. Our personal challenge has been to identify a kind of experiencing which might serve as a link, a point of connection, or the most effective avenue of entry into what Abraham Maslow once described as "the farther reaches of human nature."

Chapter 1

A leap into bodily knowing

Has it ever struck you that there really are no satisfactory *explanations* for suffering and death? Logic and reason crumble before blind catastrophes and those other senseless tragedies that litter our evolutionary journey. Stripped of all power by such occurrences, the rational mind becomes mute and helpless, like an inarticulate spectator at a funeral.

Perhaps this is because suffering, tragedy, and death really have no satisfactory intellectual explanations. Beyond all logic and reason, their true depth is rarely touched except through the body's appreciation of some deeper meaning and connectedness.

The key goal in spirituality and human evolution is to develop a consciousness potential within the *entire* human organism. Cut off from the knowing that is proper to our bodies, we lose that integral awareness through which we can resonate as living cells within a Larger Cosmic Organism.

Bio-spirituality is growing in an experience of this greater connectedness. It is a term we use to identify the *body* element in spirituality, a knowing that is beyond what reason and the brain can think. The *bio-* in bio-spirituality defines an area within our experience which we feel is an essential ingredient for any spiritual journey.

Bio- recognizes that the knowing proper to our bodies, with a small "b," is an immediate inner doorway to the gifted story of some greater At-Homeness which lies within an even Larger Body of Awareness.

Perhaps we need adversity to thrust us beyond the narrow perceptions which blind us to these broader currents. Tragedies, as well as the other mysteries of life, are never *solved* by our intellects but *resolved* in our bodies through an organic inner wisdom. Becoming lost when there are no more rational answers forces us, finally, to launch deeper into ourselves.

But what is bodily knowing? Toward what experience in ourselves must we look in order to find that special vista on some Larger Awareness? We will begin our search in this chapter by considering two questions: "How do we lose touch with bodily knowing in the first place?" and "How can we recover it without sacrificing or abandoning the obvious benefits of intellect and reason?"

As a start toward answering the first question, you might recall some examples from long ago of how you learned to block your body's knowing. As children we were all hurt by people and by circumstances. We felt scared, angry, confused, frightened, and insecure. These feelings were in our bodies, and we felt them physically. Our bodies hurt and sometimes we cried. As adults, we may not even remember some of these early, painful experiences. *But our bodies remember.* The hurt is still there, lodged deep within us.

Have you ever met people who twenty, thirty, or even fifty years after they have been wronged still *feel* exactly the same way about the aggravating person or situation? By retelling their stories they relive the entire episode again. All the old feelings are torn open once more. Their hurt has never changed or moved in any way. The old battle wounds remain unhealed.

We all know people like that. They recount their bad experiences with as much energy as if they had just happened yesterday. Without realizing it, they might have told us the same story many times before. But they launch into it once again, so intense are the feelings still generated by the retelling. They try to flush some aggravating negativity out of their systems by repeatedly recounting how they had been wronged. But it doesn't work.

What happened to many of these people and to many of us as children is that no one ever taught us *how to be in our hurt* so that it could unfold into a better place, a better feeling, and therefore into a better experience of our bodies. Usually we grew to experience negative feelings as bad, something to be avoided because they made our bodies feel bad and hurt. Most of us concluded that if we were to avoid experiencing a hurting body, then we had to avoid experiencing the kinds of feelings that made it hurt. So we adopted various strategies to avoid coming to grips with bodily knowing. Some of us learned to *distance* ourselves from our feelings. We became masters at distracting ourselves from pain; we created our own little worlds in the spaces between our dealings with other people.

But there is no way that some events in our lives won't hurt us. Feelings of anger, jealousy, fright, and guilt will sweep over us. They simply happen.

Yet as soon as they do, we usually push them away. We try to get rid of them or repress them. We seek ways to flush such painful emotions out of our systems. Anything to bring peace and calm, so our bodies will feel better.

Rarely, though, have we been taught *how to be in the hurt*, allowing it to say something about life and ourselves, letting it tell its own unique story.

Most of us *never allowed hurts to unfold*. We closed off an entire dimension of ourselves. Rather than being supported in working through our pain, the process was usually aborted. We might easily have developed a habit of denying or not listening to our feelings, and the distress in our bodies could easily have grown from this. At times, we might even have developed an attitude of not wanting to feel much of anything for fear of feeling something bad. We may have gradually closed off our ability or our need to listen to our bodies. Generally, this was done not only from fear of experiencing something bad, but also from fear of re-experiencing all the old hurts that were never allowed to unfold in the first place.

Deep down, though, our bodies know that this unprocessed experiencing is still there. Each of us instinctively realizes this, and we are usually reluctant to resurrect it. As a result, the entire area of feeling anything can become extremely risky for some people.

It is no wonder, then, that much of every day's experiencing is lived almost exclusively in our heads. Such rejection of bodily knowing eventually takes its toll, however. We suffer and break down physically and emotionally. As someone once said, mental illness is brought on not because we have "gone out of our minds" but because we are "too much in them"! We become cut off from a more integral way of knowing reality and knowing ourselves. We are cut off from the human values and perceptions rooted in our bodies that enable us to live on this planet without destroying everything around us. The origins of violence and potential planetary destruction lie deep within such alienation from ourselves.

Mother Teresa, the Nobel Peace Prize recipient, recently said something that caught our attention. She observed that society knows, in general, what to do for the hungry, the naked, and the sick. But she sensed a far more radical poverty, especially in the West. It is subtle and more difficult to transform. Food, clothing, and all the bandages in the world can never touch the widespread frustration, anxiety, loneliness, anger, and depression which permeate our culture. This requires a different kind of healing.

What makes Focusing unusual is that it creates an inner climate around our painful and frightening issues that is different from the climate we generally fall into with problems and difficulties. Normally, we feel bad about things we don't like in ourselves. We are sometimes ashamed, feel guilty, annoyed, or impatient. We hold at arm's length and try to control what we cannot accept. Focusing invites us to relate in a different way to what we perceive as unloveable in ourselves.

"Can I find some way to be a little more *friendly* with my feelings that are so hard to deal with?" This is a vital element in the Focusing process. Being friendly usually doesn't solve the problem, at least not right away. But it is a special way of being more gentle, more open, less argumentative, and more kind with a hurting place in ourselves. This allows us, sometimes for the very first time, to really feel our problem as we carry it in a bodily way. Most of us only feel our uncomfortableness with a problem or our need to control it. Rarely, however, do we experience what it is like deliberately and consciously to be *in* the body's sense of negative issues without immediately being pressured either to control or eliminate whatever hurting, scary, or other feelings are there. This openness to bodily knowing within the Focusing process sets the stage for real and sometimes dramatic change as hurting places are allowed to unfold.

This brings us to our second question: "How can we recover a more integral connection with bodily knowing?"

Several years ago during a workshop the two of us conducted with Dr. Eugene Gendlin, one of our participants raised a question about negative hurts and feelings.

Her point was that she found it relatively easy to be present to positive feelings of joy, excitement, love, tenderness, curiosity, and so on. But anger, depression, guilt, loneliness, frustration, and a desire for revenge—these she found more difficult.

Dr. Gendlin's response challenged her to adopt a new perspective. He replied: "You must learn to be with your negative feeling *as you would be with a hurting child."*

The image was graphic. To sit down with hostility, fear, or grief, and deliberately put your arm around something in yourself which for years you might have held at arm's length was quite a challenge. Almost like going to bed with the devil!

This called to mind tales of the Senoi, an isolated jungle folk who live on the Malay Peninsula. Parents in this tribe have a marvelous way of counseling their children when the little ones have nightmares. Rather than just comforting them after such a frightening experience, the parents open another possibility by suggesting: "Oh, that's an opportunity. It's really the best kind of dream you can have!"

The child, obviously, doesn't think it was so nice. Nightmares of falling, for example, are ordinarily very scary. But the mother and father persist: "When you fall in a dream, you're really falling into a *deeper place in yourself.* It is the place from which a Great Spirit speaks. Someday you will recall these words right inside your dream. Then, letting yourself go into this fearful adventure, you will come face to face with a wonderful surprise!"

The message of these examples, both in our workshop and in the Senoi approach to dreams is essentially the same. Allow yourself to be fully in the bodily knowing of your unacceptable, fearful experience, and it will unfold a surprising story—usually quite different from what reason might lead you to expect.

During one of our recent workshops we mentioned the Senoi and their approach to dreams. After the session a woman came forward, excited at what she had heard and wanting to share a similar experience. As a child she had always been told that if she failed to awaken before reaching the bottom of her dream fall, she would die! Later, as an adult, she endured a prolonged period during which she experienced many nightmares of falling. She had dreams from which she would awaken terrified with her heart pounding.

One night, however, as the familiar nightmare returned and she found herself beginning to fall, she made the deliberate decision *inside her dream* to let go and allow herself to drop. She recalled being over some European village. Clearly visible below her were the tiled roofs of homes and buildings nestled together in a narrow valley. The ground rushed up toward her at a dizzying pace. All the while she knew she could stop this terrible experience by just waking up. The temptation was great to do so. "The roofs got closer and closer," she said. "The ground came up faster and faster." "And finally," she exclaimed, "I hit!" Then, turning her eyes wide with amazement, she asked: "Can you guess what happened?"

"I bounced! A glorious, easy, airy, delight-filled bounce. But even more important," she confided, "up to the present day I have *never again* experienced that terrible nightmare!"

She had *become* her falling. By *owning* this dimension of her being, *allowing* the bodily felt sense of it to unfold, she had stumbled upon a surprising doorway. It was an entry point of transformation in the way her body carried a hurting past experience.

For a moment now, put yourself in the place of a Senoi child who has just emerged from a nightmare. The thought of going back and *letting go* into a dream fall rather than fighting to gain control of or stopping your descent through waking up would be a terrifying prospect, wouldn't it?

Or, would it? Recall your worst nightmare. Are you perhaps just a little intrigued at what might have happened had you been able to just *let go* in such a situation and not try to control or escape?

The transition to such risk-taking, however, is rarely

easy. The New Testament speaks of *metanoia* — conversion. A step beyond control. It is often frightening, but it's challenging as well. Conversion leads gradually toward possessing more and more of your self! It involves letting go of controls which hold you to a narrow and often confining experience. There is the challenge of a hidden surprise. A gift. A grace waiting in the uncertainty of that overpowering darkness from which we generally shield ourselves.

We recall another dream we once shared between the two of us. In this particular nightmare, Peter was suddenly confronted by a terrifying, bearded man. A powerful Old Testament–type figure robed in a cloak and filled with wrath who glared and shouted like a threatening Ayatollah.

Pete's initial reaction was one of traumatic fear and a desperate effort to flee. But then he stopped short, and recalled within his own dream the story about the Senoi.

At that point he too deliberately turned, and with a good deal of inner trembling he slowly advanced toward what appeared to be certain harm. The closer he approached, the angrier the bearded figure became. The intensity of his rage was almost more than Pete could bear. But his determination held. Saying nothing, he walked forward until he was face to face with the figure. Then came the surprise.

Without any warning this terrifying apparition suddenly broke down and began to weep; it shriveled up at the same time into a very little and feeble old man. It was a stunning experience. One which Peter will never forget.

The important point here is not "What does the dream mean?" Our reason for recalling these vivid episodes is to illustrate a letting go of the reins that must be practiced regularly *while a person is fully awake and alert*. It is a counter culture commitment to the sometimes frightening act of consciously letting ourselves fall into our entire organism's awareness of each moment.

Dreams like these made us wonder. Could there be a deliberate, wide-awake way to *position* ourselves so that we could be drawn inside whatever was real, even though it was fearful or difficult?

Is it not strange that most of us resist this *letting go* into what our bodies know about something? We are reluctant to try anything beyond the mind's logical, reasoned approach to problem solving. We avoid this alternate path, finding any excuse to distract ourselves from growing quiet and attending to what our whole being, especially our bodies, can tell us about how things are right now.

Few of us believe that such bodily knowing can express an awesome invitation to the benevolent wisdom and grace of the cosmos. It is frightening to let go of the reins. Most people suffer such vulnerability only as a desperate last resort. We doubt the possibility of survival. Resurrection in such circumstances is quite literally *beyond* reason.

Yet there is wisdom in our bodies! A sure-footed sense for deeper meaning, purpose, and direction. But this wisdom lies behind an obscuring veil within ourselves. Perhaps it is like a screen falling at the farther edge of reason. Possibly our mind itself is the veil. No matter what, the letting go required to pass beyond this barrier contradicts all of our cultural conditioning and educational programming.

This is because human transformation depends upon far more than information. The critical factor for change is not *understanding* but an experience of give, shift, or *movement* in the bodily awareness of a problem or life situation. This is not seeing new things; it's a new way of seeing! It is an experience of inner *release*. This is what counts and what makes real change in awareness possible.

The difficulty, of course, is that this kind of release always flies with wings of unpredictability. It seldom arrives on schedule. It has an air of haphazardness and it eludes programmed control; it comes more like a *gift*, a grace.

We don't *make* the human story unfold. Our bodily-felt carrying of this next step cannot be hurried along through pre-planned control and engineering. It must be *allowed* to come into existence.

Loosening the reins of this control and letting ourselves experience such graced wisdom are two essential ingredients of bio-spirituality. They open a way of being in ordinary awareness, scary or joyful, which allows the shadowy places as well as the happy ones to tell their stories. Here, finally, we can find a doorway into a realm of greater freedom and a sense for a Larger At-Homeness that may help us avoid the perilous shoals of potential nuclear holocaust.

Let us turn, then, to the practical details of what we will now call *the art of allowing.*

Chapter 2

Learning to focus

Practical steps
toward the art of allowing

What does it feel like inside to let go of the reins? What part of you gets involved? Toward what kind of experiencing is it best to direct your attention? What can you do? What can you *not* do to support an unfolding of your own bio-spiritual perspective? Let's turn now to some practical steps in the art of allowing.

In this chapter we will describe our approach to Focusing. After that we will begin to sketch a broader vision, situating the art of allowing within a framework of evolutionary spirituality. We will probe that inviting frontier in ourselves which Teilhard de Chardin sought to describe. Ultimately we want to peer into the depth of a bio-spirituality which draws both us and our world into a ripening Mystery of cosmic congruence.

But first we must learn a method or an approach to bodily knowing. Taking one step at a time then, let's reconsider those hurts we described in Chapter 1, hurts which our bodies can never forget.

So many people simply go around in circles with their negative feelings. Having never learned to get beneath an emotion into the wider bodily felt sense of a problem, they remain locked in self-defeating patterns. Instead of on-going change that would refresh their inner landscapes, the same stale emotional responses recur with frustrating regularity. These people live with more or less rigid, pre-programmed *reactions* to specific situations and people. Given a particular stimulus, they always feel the *same kind* of anger, the same resentful hurt, or the same re-curring sense of inferiority. A well-worn record plays over and over again. There is no bodily felt release within which to experience change. There is no inner *resolution* of their tiresome, debilitating response.

From a therapeutic point of view, Eugene Gendlin's unique contribution has been to show that surface emo-tions, whether positive or negative, are directly tied to a more rudimentary *felt sense* of how a particular issue is carried in the body. Successful therapy has something to do with a refreshing release in this area of experiencing.

Gendlin found meaning beyond the mind. There is *felt* meaning as well, a meaning that is known and carried in the body. This meaning is different from that which we think. Not that such *bodily* meaning is unintelligible, it just *behaves* differently from the meanings that we can conceptualize.

This remains a rather vague area for most of us. We can usually identify our more obvious feelings and emo-tions. But the deeper felt meanings tied in with such emo-tions are less readily available to our ordinary awareness. At least we don't *attend* to them with the same facility and discipline with which we solve practical everyday problems.

Words like *fear, anger, resentment,* and *joy* say some-thing in general about certain feelings which we all have. These words are useful tools for communication. But the universal term *anger* never completely describes the uniquely personal flavor of *my* anger. *Anger* is a generic word. It refers to anger in general, just as *flower* names the blossom of any plant without specifying that which differentiates it as totally unique—*this* red rosebud.

My anger is always more than just anger in general. It has a specific *texture* which includes an initially nameless, somewhat tangled mass of inner, bodily felt meaning that colors *this* anger as uniquely my own. The more readily observable outburst of emotion is only the tip of an iceberg.

Eugene Gendlin has referred to the broader substratum beneath this visible tip as a *felt sense*. This term embraces a wider, initially nebulous meaning that is felt rather than conceptualized in our awareness. It is called *felt* because it is felt in the body. It is called *sense,* not like the five senses, but more like *the sense of something* or *he makes good sense. Sense,* here, is a meaning word. It is a meaning that is felt—as yet unclear and vague. A meaning prior to symbolization.

As Gendlin points out, to feel "unaccountably uncomfortable" means you are aware of more in your body than you can think in your mind. That is a felt sense, and it is always more than what you may have immediate words or rational explanations for. In fact, it is often a clear sign of a *felt sense* when you definitely experience something without yet having the right word or symbol for it.

The felt sense, then, is rarely reason-logical. It is rather body-logical. Its meaning will not fit easily into the categories of cause and effect. The felt sense exhibits surprising twists and turns; it almost seems to have a different function than the meanings we think with our minds. This is why we said earlier that it behaves differently.

As an example, we recall one workshop in which a woman began to focus, and immediately she felt overwhelmed by sadness and tears without in any way knowing why or what this was all about. Her body felt sadness, yet her mind could in no way understand or explain why she had such a feeling. She needed time to be with this felt sense until it could unfold a deeper story. The story, it turned out, was quite different from what she consciously thought about certain issues in her life. Her body realized something that she had never allowed herself to become aware of in her head.

The felt sense, then, does not seem to be directed toward solutions in our intellects but toward a *resolution* in the way our bodies carry certain issues and concerns in our lives. Its function has something to do with a special movement or release within the realm of organismic rather than exclusively mental knowing.

But what is this movement, and how does it take place? What triggers this transformation?

In pursuing this elusive resolution, Dr. Gendlin decided not to work directly with surface emotions. Rather, using the procedure called Focusing, he found that a person could be taught to move his or her awareness *through* an emotion deeper into the bodily felt awareness of a problem. The more easily identifiable surface emotion is *not* the principal lever that facilitates a change. It represents, rather, a vital *doorway* into that realm of experiencing where change can occur—much like the nightmare for the Senoi child revealed an unexpected depth of spirit.

What, then, are the basic instructions for Focusing? Since it is an art that can only be fully appreciated in the actual doing of it, our goal in the following pages is not to offer a practical manual on how to focus. This has already been done by Dr. Gendlin in his book called *Focusing*.[1]

We find that the technique aspect of Focusing is best learned from someone who is experienced in the method and who regularly practices it in his or her life. Books or manuals about Focusing can be useful tools in this learning process. They are especially helpful, and in some instances may even substitute for a good teacher, when the learner knows how to make that vital leap between information on the printed page and what is actually occuring within his or her own experience. When a person instinctively *knows* what an author is writing about, not as information but through a sense of *having been there themselves*—then learning can go forward. If this should happen in your reading of what follows, so much the better. But we set a more modest goal for ourselves.

We simply want to provide you with some appreciation for how your inner story might unfold. We wish to heighten your awareness of how your body speaks its own unique language, and how destructive patterns of feeling can be resolved. These pages are primarily an invitation to look further into yourself.

If anything, our aim is motivational. By carefully attending to certain experiences you could be led toward that gifted inner stream where the sense for being bodily alive in some Larger Process can unfold. This broader bio-spiritual enterprise is our principal concern. Let's consider, then, the process of Focusing as one promising approach to this inviting inner world.

There are certain steps which anyone can follow when first learning to focus. These steps are taught in different ways by different teachers. What we now wish to share is the way *we* teach Focusing. It is not the only way. We just find that it has worked well for the two of us. Once a person achieves a certain familiarity with the process, some of the initial steps may occasionally be dropped. We encourage beginners to go through the entire series, however, because it provides a useful framework within which to learn one's own unique pattern and language of unfolding.

Our approach in this chapter will be to describe each step of Focusing and then to comment on it in some detail. We will share experiences and examples which we find help us and our workshop participants learn to Focus. Once we have completed this more lengthy description, we will summarize at the end of the book, the basic steps so that anyone may readily use them either when Focusing alone or when helping someone else.

We should note here that Focusing can be greatly facilitated by the caring presence of another person. This must, however, be a presence which never seeks to intrude or to force any predetermined agenda on the one

Focusing. A good facilitator simply "walks along" with the focuser, providing support and minimal assistance for the direction and the surprise that can emerge from within the person who is actually doing the Focusing.

Let's turn, then, to the steps involved in this process. We call the first step *Finding a Space by Taking an Inventory*.

A person usually begins Focusing by taking a moment to step back from the ongoing rush of thinking and emotion which fills so much of every day. This is like a quick breather which serves as a prelude to what follows next. This initial moment is perhaps best understood by realizing what it is *not*. It is not relaxing! It is not seeking some deep place for meditation and quiet or a brief escape.

If something is bothering you, if you have a nagging inner felt sense clamoring for attention, you don't want to lose it or dull it by first getting nice and comfortable. No. The initial stepping back is meant to *sharpen* any bodily awareness that may be there ready to be focused upon.

What you seek in this opening moment of Focusing is to back off from the usually jumbled stream of feelings and thoughts inside of you so that you are not overwhelmed by confusion. You don't back away from what needs to be focused upon; you back away from *the mixing up* of that with a whole lot of other things that may currently be occupying your attention.

What you want to do in this opening moment is allow your attention to drop downward into the feeling part of yourself. Sometimes it helps just to close your eyes and ask yourself something like this: "How am I right now?" Let the answer to that question rise from deep within you, not as a thinking but as a feeling. Give yourself a moment to break away from your ordinary problem-solving, rational, worrying self, and just attend to your body's knowing right now.

While growing quiet inside, let your attention settle

toward the center of your body—the solar plexus region. We encourage people to include awareness of this area in their bodies right at the beginning of Focusing because it often helps them notice more easily how their bodies are carrying life issues. After a few moments of turning your awareness inward in this way, ask yourself the following question: "Is there anything keeping me from feeling really good right now?"

Sit with that question for a while and see what comes.

The question may cause an image to pop into your head or a memory to return. Perhaps a hunch may come forward. Something that has been bothering you may finally surface, or a queasy feeling might arise in your stomach. Notice, in particular, your inner response to the question. How does your body carry whatever keeps you from feeling really good right now? For example, is there a tightness in your chest? Perhaps, an aching loneliness? Maybe you notice a vague feeling of being chained down, suffocating, or always being rushed by the pace of your life. Allow yourself a few moments to notice the felt sense side of whatever comes in response to that question.

Once you have identified something, don't try to do anything with it. Don't spend time feeling bad about it, trying to solve it, or figuring it out. Just notice whatever comes. Then, if you can, gently put it aside for the time being.

Give yourself a moment in which to sense what it feels like to set this down beside you and not be carrying it within you. Then, if you can do this, ask yourself another question: "If this were all resolved, would there be anything else between me and feeling really fine right now?"

It may be that the first feeling that comes is so painful or up front that you can't set it aside and continue. If that happens, then go on to what we will call Step Number Three in the Focusing process. Usually, however, if what comes up is not all that preoccupying, it can be set aside temporarily in order to see whether something else lies between you and feeling really good at that moment.

Some interesting things can happen when you ask the further question: "If this were all resolved, would there be anything else between me and feeling fine right now?" Occasionally, an unexpected bodily carrying of an additional issue will emerge when you ask this question. Generally, when you pose the first question about what's keeping you from feeling really good right now, your body's sense for some *current* concern will surface. Not always, of course, but more often than not. Then when this is momentarily set aside, there is room for more subtle shades of body awareness to emerge. Awareness, we might add, which is not always dark or difficult or bad. An unrealized excitement can often surface. You may occasionally be surprised by more profound life issues that have gotten lost in the flurry of daily activities.

What you are doing in this unusual bodily felt inventory is gradually working your way toward an open space in yourself which lies on the other side of all the felt issues which remain unresolved at this time. Many people who eventually reach that space often find that it opens into an important spiritual experience for them. They discover a kind of inner widening of self. Having set down, for a moment, their burden of difficult things, they detect a glimmer of some spiritual "more" which momentarily refreshes their inner being.

But this is *not* the immediate goal of the first step in Focusing. If it should happen, that's good. But what we are about is something quite different. At this early point in the Focusing process, we simply want to give our bodies a chance to surface the largely unnoticed *carrying* of life which lies within us at every waking moment.

So some people may find it helpful to repeat several times: "If this were all resolved, then could I feel really fine right now, or would there still be something between me and feeling OK?" As often as some further issue arises, notice it, then gently set it aside to see if anything else wants to come forward. In this way you will be taking an inventory in which your goal is nothing more than to *identify* what is there without attempting to *do* anything with it.

Sometimes when people ask the first question: "Is anything keeping me from feeling really good right now?" the answer may be "No!" That's a special moment for anyone if it should happen. No negative or unresolved body feeling surfaces to claim our attention. Whenever this happens, you can then ask: "Are there any other things in my life right now, not necessarily problems, that it would be good to get in touch with?" This is also a question you may ask after you've noticed and set aside whatever keeps you from feeling really good right now.

This second part of your inventory provides an opportunity to review other important issues in your life in addition to the more vague or troublesome feelings which may have surfaced initially. It is not always necessary to ask this further question, unless, of course, you find that nothing particularly bothersome came into your awareness when you first checked to see if anything stood between you and feeling really good right now.

What this further question does, if you use it, is to allow a wider range of issues, feelings, and concerns— both positive and negative— to come forward and identify themselves. Once again, the goal is not to begin fretting over worrisome items in your line-up. This is simply an opportunity to take stock of what is there. You're conducting an *inventory*—nothing more, nothing less.

One suggestion we always make to participants in our workshops, though, is to be on the lookout for unexpected elements that may pop into their inventories by surprise. Most of the time we think we know what our primary issues, problems, and concerns are. But the questions we ask in setting the stage for Focusing involve far more than a rational exercise done with our heads. We must remain open for our body's knowing to come in and suggest things. After a little practice, you'll gradually recognize subtle ways in which this occurs.

Usually what happens is that some uninvited element flies by on the periphery of your consciousness. It may be an image, the memory of some painful or embarrassing situation, or perhaps an unexpected anticipation of something that will happen tomorrow. You must be alert to catch these little surprises as they flit by on the edge of your awareness.

Do you know what peripheral vision is like? Catching some movement out of the corner of your eye. The appearance of bodily knowing is often like that. But when you have spent years attending primarily to what can be thought in your mind, it's easy to miss these marginal clues. They slip by without being noticed.

Soon, however, as you begin to recognize them, and especially as you discover how they can really be treasures leading toward a deeper resolution in bodily knowing, you will value them and attend more carefully to their appearance.

Moreover, you'll occasionally find random details popping into your awareness which seem to have little connection with anything either at a thinking or a body-feeling level. First check to see if they have a *feeling of importance*. If not, just let them slip by. Should they be really significant and you lose them, they'll eventually come back.

The real effort in this first step must be to remain open to whatever seems to be *most up front* for you right now in your life. This can include items that are big or small, long-term or relatively recent, good or bad. Remember that the inventory is not just picking out problems and hurts. It's allowing *anything* that happens to have a kind of here-and-now organismic energy to come forward and be recognized. This can include major life decisions and situations, small pinpricks and bright spots that have occurred in the last day, or little surprises that come uninvited as through from nowhere.

The point of this first step in Focusing is not to make an exhaustive catalogue of every possible memory, hurt, or expectation that might figure in to your current sense of self. Try to regard this initial exercise like the cream that used to rise to the top of the old milk bottles. You're just trying to get the main things, the cream off the top. Should you miss something, don't worry about it. If it's really important, it will come up again some other time.

There is an amazing wisdom within the human organism. It knows more about the "way home to ourselves" than we can ever think in our heads. It knows where all the inner blockages are that stand in the way of growing, and it has enough sense to move the "big ones" forward in their proper time and sequence so that a resolution may occur.

Finding a Space by Taking an Inventory provides your body with a chance to speak. It lets whatever lies between you and some larger picture come to the surface and identify itself. The surprising thing, however, is that the very items which rise into awareness as apparent obstacles and stumbling blocks to spiritual unfolding are, in fact, your most privileged pathways into the Larger Mystery. In this first step of Focusing *you identify doorways!* All those feelings and felt meanings which stand between you and a more open inner space actually contain your body's potential for being drawn further forward into a vast evolutionary unfolding.

None of us can ever *think* our way into bio-spiritual awareness. We are rather drawn forward along a path of more integral bodily knowing.

Finally, it helps to look at this first step in Focusing with a generous amount of flexibility. If during the course of your inventory you should come upon something which stands out with a vibrancy and energy that clamors for immediate attention, then maybe that's what you should be with for now. Don't feel compelled to *finish* your inventory before coming back to this matter.

One additional point, too, about that more open inner space, the "feeling really good right now" which lies on the other side of all the bodily-felt obstacles in between.

Remember that this space is a developmental experience. It will be different for different people. It will even be different for the same person at different times.

Sometimes the inner space and good feeling will be nothing more than tension reduction. For a person in physical pain, simply to have the agony stop or diminish somewhat is enough. It is a place of rest, a gratifying break in what may be a very trying ordeal. At other times, however, the space may turn into an awe-inspiring place of wonder, a spiritual vista point.

What is important about such a space is that it can provide a bodily-felt experience which reveals that there is more to who you are than the current pain or malaise to which your attention may be narrowed. This is extremely important, especially for someone who usually lives with a constricted sense of self. Such a person desperately needs to find a place of fresh air deep inside.

Even though time may elapse before you actually become congruent with such an experience, it is important to touch it *at least as promise!* Finding this space of feeling good within yourself can serve as a beacon of hope. It can be a light beyond the many obstacles which still stand in the path of finding a way through to some positive core experience. We are reminded of those magnificent lines which close the Genesis creation narrative: "And God saw everything that he had made, *and behold it was very good.*" (*Gen. 1:31, RSV,* emphasis ours) All of us continually seek a bodily-felt sense of that *goodness* which lies at the core of our being. Finding a Space by Taking an Inventory can be an important step on this journey into ourselves. Let's now turn to what comes next.

We call the second step of Focusing *Feeling Which One Is Number One.* What you do at this point is to return to the various issues you have identified thus far. Passing before each of them, you now try to gain some feeling for which item stands out as Number One for you *at this precise moment.* Which is the one to spend time with now?

What draws you to itself in such a way that you *know* this is the one to focus on?

We emphasize the first word in our description of this step: *Feeling* which is Number One.

Feeling! The discernment which you make at this point is never one of logical judgment or evaluation. It must not be a decision based upon that you think *ought* to be focused upon at this time. No. Take your cue from the inherent power or energy that an item may have for you in this particular moment.

That's why it is often good to ask yourself *feeling questions* like: "Which one is the warmest, the heaviest, the most uncomfortable, the most pressing, the most exciting, and so on." Think of this not as a rational selection process but more like *taking the temperature* of each bodily felt sense until you find one which stands out above all the others.

We had an interesting experience with a participant in one of our workshops which illustrates this point. A man had come to the weekend workshop determined to spend time working on his feelings about his marriage. His agenda was all laid out in advance. But when, during Focusing, he risked allowing his entire organism to reveal what was Number One, something unexpected happened. He realized that what was most up front, apparently, was not at all what he had planned to work on. Rather, it was *his fear of Focusing!* The surprising thing, however, was that when he sat with this issue, allowing it time to symbolize itself, he was also blessed with more resolution in the marriage relationship than he ever would have experienced had he tried to force this earlier agenda upon his bodily knowing.

It helps, then, at this stage in the Focusing process to set all your *oughts* and pre-planned agenda aside. Sometimes the inconsequential, the peripheral, the unexpected becomes your doorway to change.

Recall what we said earlier about felt meaning. It *behaves* differently. It is not mind-logical. There is no way to force a resolution in bodily knowing. You can sometimes override feelings with various coping devices and behavior modification. But lasting change is a gift from within the flow of your own story. Focusing provides an opportunity for such a grace to appear.

If there can be a reverent "sitting down beside" the items of our inventory, then one of them in some uniquely personal fashion will signal a primacy over all the others—at least for now.

Obviously, when you are clearly upset, you *know* right away without any inventory what is Number One. At those times you can simply dispense with these early steps. You can ask yourself: "How am I right now?" With little hesitation the felt sense of that moment will usually come crashing into awareness.

The inventory, however, can be helpful in quieter times. It's also useful when there is such a turmoil of hurting and conflict that sorting things out a bit will help to bring your attention to bear on what lies within. Use whatever approach seems right at any given moment.

Once you have been able to *feel* Number One, you are then ready to move on to the third step. This involves asking a very important question.

Is It OK to Be With This? It is a simple request designed to respect freedom, and it never forces you beyond the control which may be necessary at any given point in your life.

Sometimes what surfaces as Number One may be, for the beginner, too frightening to be with. Maybe it's a long-term, deep-rooted experience, so painful that any proximity is too much to bear. There is usually a great deal of initial fear and healthy scepticism about getting involved with this kind of hurt in ourselves. Perhaps every past attempt to work with pain has resulted in more pain or simply a wallowing in misery. If so, there is usually no positive back-up experience to support risking such an approach again.

Focusing, however, is a radically different way of being with such a difficult blockage in ourselves. But the beginner doesn't yet know this, and he or she should never rashly push past defenses set up to protect against the inner anguish of getting too close. Time and experience will eventually show that this process allows even the deepest kinds of hurt to unfold.

We recall a humorous incident which occured during a workshop which included among the participants a trained therapist who regularly used Focusing in her own life and professional practice. The timing of this workshop happened to coincide with her own working through a rather painful experience in her life. She was Focusing in a small practice group with others who were just beginning to Focus for the first time. Pete, the facilitator, asked the standard question: "Is it OK to be with all that?" The question was asked as much for the teaching value it had for the rest of the group as for the person to whom it was directed. There was a long pause as the woman struggled back from the depth of her own painful felt sense. Then, cocking her head to the side, she opened one eye and with an exquisitely knowing smile said: "I can be with *any-thing!*"

Experience in Focusing always leads beyond the need for permission to go ahead. But in the beginning it is a salutary check point.

What happens, though, if the answer is "No"? What if your sense for Number One is such that you don't want to get within a country mile of it? Then what can you do?

Whenever the Number One item is simply too much to be with for now, you must respect the need for distance. Then try an alternate approach. Open another possibility by asking yourself: "Is it OK to be with the feeling of not wanting to get into all this right now?" Can you Focus on your being afraid of it, too tired to face it, or whatever else happens to express your unique "No" response in such a situation?

Do you see what you're doing by taking this route? You are, first of all, continuing to remain with what is real at the moment; namely, an unwillingness to get involved with this Number One. But remember, all this hanging back has a bodily felt sense associated with it. It's not the big one, but it is an integral part of getting close to this area of major blockage. It is equally part of your process. So, go with it.

By taking this kind of approach you remain within the stream of *real* experiencing without having to tackle your big problem head on. This usually turns out to be a "coming in the back door" on the main issue. Gradually, after a while, you wind your way into it at your own pace.

It might help you to think of your rich inner world of bodily felt meaning as a large embroidered tapestry. Something like one of those magnificent wall hangings you find in museums. Now imagine that a thread comes loose somewhere on the tapestry. If you pull that thread and follow its unravelling, it will eventually cross other threads that lead into every part of the picture. No matter where you jump in, the thread you follow at that point will sooner or later connect with every important item in the total design.

Focusing is like that! You may begin at some inconsequential little sketch in an obscure corner of the tapestry that is your inner landscape of felt meaning, but eventually you will be drawn through to everything that is inside you! The critical point, however, is *finding the first loose thread!* That's what your inventory and getting the feel of Number One allows you to do. It gives your body a chance to point the way. The threads, remember, are rarely where we *think* they *should* be. They are the loose ends of life, the unfinished in ourselves where doorways yet remain to be opened.

It is important to realize when Focusing that you never play games with yourself. The goal here is more than just coping with bad situations. It is an inner positioning for the gifted possibility of genuine change. You are seeking bodily-felt resolution in the way you carry some problem or issue. This is not just a novel way to feel good for a while. It's not just snatching a bit of rest before lifting again the burdens you wake up with each morning. To Focus means to risk the possibility that each burden may have a chance to tell its own story and in the telling might be changed from within.

There are many doorways leading into this resolution in bodily knowing. It is important to find the one which seems most appropriate for you at any given moment. The guiding principle is always to go with some bodily felt sense that you can touch right now. If it is OK to be with your Number One, even though it might be a little scary, then go with it. If not, then go with *the being scared* about getting into it.

Should you find that your being with a particularly difficult Number One eventually becomes too scary and you want to stop, remember that *you are always the one in charge*. If you want to stop, stop! Or, better, switch over to: "Now this is getting too difficult to get into." See if you can be with that fear of going further, letting it tell its story. Eventually, as you travel along on your inner journey, learning its mysterious and sometimes surprising ways, you, too, may be blessed with that marvelous inner liberation: "I can be with *anything!*"

There is an unexpected resource within the flesh and sinew of bodily knowing. A bio-spiritual aliveness which can draw you well beyond fear into the vitalizing inner sense for *being a new creation!* But we are getting ahead of ourselves.

Once it is OK to be with a felt sense of Number One, then what? We have tried various ways of describing the fourth step in Focusing as we teach it. *Letting Go into It; Just Being In It; Sensing the Whole of It.* Here, the inner stance is not one of trying to figure something out. Thinking is set aside. Reason is appropriate for other tasks, but not for this one. One tries, instead, to remain *inside* the felt sense of Number One.

Have you ever suffered a severe headache or the pain of an arthritic joint? Do you know the inner experience as you try to *distance* yourself from that kind of suffering?

The soreness becomes almost an alien force, something that is not you, that attacks you. You try to hold the pain at arm's length, trying to keep it *outside* of your "you." There is an inner shrinking back from the pain, from the soreness that is right within your own body. Perhaps you know something of this attempted dissociation.

But have you ever tried the exact opposite? Moving right into the middle of your pain? Being *inside it* instead of struggling to separate yourself from it. Just letting go into it. Surprises can sometimes occur when you do this.

In the first chapter we wrote about being *friendly* with difficult feelings and issues. Step four in Focusing is a special way of getting beyond the practice of holding what hurts you at arm's length. If the main thing you're in touch with about a painful feeling or situation is that you don't like it or wish it would go away, then you always remain one step removed from the actual feeling that needs to change. Transformation becomes possible to the extent that you directly touch your felt carrying of an issue and not just your negative feelings about it. This encourages an attitude of open listening to what is really inside you, the hurt, confusion, bitterness, longing, or whatever.

We encourage those who attend our workshops to look for *concrete images* that can help them move beyond always holding what is troublesome at arm's length. Many find Dr. Gendlin's suggestion helpful: imagining that they are holding a painful issue on their lap just as they might hold a hurting child. Others, for whom this is too much, find it helpful to imagine themselves simply resting their hand on whatever hurts inside; this allows a different relationship to emerge. Some find it necessary to locate what bothers them at a distance from themselves, for example, across the room or just outside the door. Such distancing sometimes makes it possible to experience the felt sense of an issue that has been avoided because it is so painful, frightening, confusing, or whatever.

Concrete imaging can be helpful because it breaks patterns and creates a different climate around an issue you don't like or have been avoiding inside yourself. This makes it easier, then, to let go into how the issue actually feels in your body. We all tend, in some way, to block out our negative felt sensing. This is usually unintentional, but it can easily become habitual. Using "friendly" imagery helps us be more open inside, allowing hurting places to tell their stories. As this happens, our bodily felt carrying of some painful memory, situation, or feeling can then begin to change.

One humorous illustration of "Letting go into it" comes from our workshop instructions. You know what it's like when you're out walking and it begins to rain. You usually don't want to get wet, do you? So you pull your clothes around you, tighten up your muscles, sometimes you even screw up your face a bit. You try to keep the rain and all that wetness outside of you.

Carry this experience a bit further. Have you ever found yourself caught in an absolute downpour where there was no escape? At first you tried to stay dry, fighting against the wet. But it soon became hopeless. You could feel the water dripping under your collar. Your shoes started to squish inside. Everything eventually gets absolutely soaked all the way through.

At this point, have you ever thought, "Oh, what the heck!" and deliberately *let go of trying to stay dry?* Then you know what it feels like just to walk in the rain. You relax and sometimes even enjoy it, don't you? You let go! You stop tightening up inside. Your face relaxes.

Now and then you run into people like that on busy streets during a downpour. Everyone else is rushing along, staying tight, and trying to keep the wet out, and here comes this person down the sidewalk with no umbrella, soaked through to the skin, yet sauntering along as if it were a beautiful spring day. You *notice* such people, don't you? They stand out. They sometimes even make you feel a little angry or envious.

Perhaps they're crazy! That's always a possibility. But there's something in their behavior that you would like to imitate, wouldn't you? Nobody likes to walk around all tense with their face screwed up in a knot. We all want to relax and let go into our environment.

The fourth step in Focusing is something like that. It is letting go into the full, rich felt sense of whatever rises up from within us, not holding it at arm's length or in some way keeping it *outside* our sense of self. There is no tightening up against it, as we usually tighten up against getting wet or getting hurt.

This is just being present in the felt sense, as it is, without trying to figure it out with our heads. It's like being at the beach soaking up the sun or the sound of the waves. We don't hold these outside ourselves. If anything, we enfold them into ourselves, letting them penetrate us. It's like *being in* sports or jogging, where one moves beyond thinking and technique to relishing the sheer physical movement, grace, balance, and inner sense of well-being. We don't *think* sun, waves, or movement. We somehow become them. Letting go into a felt sense is something like that.

We find it helpful in our workshops to have participants recall special moments and memories when they really were *in* some experience without thinking or trying to figure it out. Our approach, then, is to ask: "How was your body during that experience?" "What happened to your mind?" Take a moment right now to recall some such experience yourself.

In response to such questions we have often had people say: "My body felt as though all its pores were open. It was relaxed, floating, still. My mind, though, was *out to lunch!* It just wasn't thinking or trying to figure things out."

By carefully attending to how you are inside during such moments, you can get a better feel for what this step in the Focusing process is all about. The letting go, the being in a felt sense is *beyond* thinking about it. It embraces a bodily knowing which carries awareness inward in a way that thinking can never do.

Have you ever noticed how thinking always remains *outside* of that which is thought? It's the difference between subject and object. We think *about* something. We reason from cause to effect. Even when we think about ourselves, we take a stand outside of that which we think about. That's why reason can never make a tight, hurting inner place unbend! It can't get *inside* it. Solutions in the mind are never the same as a resolution in bodily knowing. Reason always remains *outside* of the hurt which it thinks about. This place may only be entered as the Senoi child was drawn to enter the dream.

Through Focusing, however, a person can finally approach this profound *interiority*. Moving beyond solutions, one finds a realm where *we are carried* more than we carry. We are led as much beyond reason and control as the risk of being inside pain and wetness leads us beyond the way we ordinarily act in our everyday lives. It is like letting go into the challenge of a dream-fall in order to be carried *through* the barrier of forever remaining outside what is—*outside our True Self!*

Letting go into a felt sense opens a radically different world within human knowing. Those who risk it experience a kind of neo-Copernican revolution. It's like waking up one morning and knowing for the first time that the sun doesn't go around the earth, even though it looks like it does! It is a shocking, yet liberating discovery.

Letting go into the felt sense marks a point of no return in the Focusing process. It's like crossing a great divide. It's a troublesome point for many, demanding commitment and what can only be called *a believing!* It takes faith to remain in the felt sense, not tampering or fiddling with it, just being there *in it* until it speaks. If you can do this, you're ready for the fifth and final step in Focusing.

Allowing It to Express Itself. Given time and a faithful remaining in the felt sense without trying to control it or force it in any way, the inner felt meaning will eventually express itself. Sometimes a word or picture will suddenly appear which says what this is all about. It will often be a spontaneous image. Occasionally there will be tears or an irrepressible giggling. Some tangible symbol will eventually arrive, often with a tinge of surprise.

You immediately know the appropriateness or accuracy of a symbol by the distinct sense of inner release you feel in your body. This is the *resolution*. It's an embodied "Yes!" which *always* feels good. This is the "felt shift" Gendlin has identified. It occurs in the gifted coming together of symbol and felt sense within your awareness. The process moves forward one more step. You sense an inner movement in your body.

Symbols which arise spontaneously are always different from those you deliberately think. The latter are rarely accompanied by any felt shift. Reason, as we said earlier, remains outside the hurt, outside the felt sense. But symbols that apparently come from nowhere, often by surprise, are usually accompanied by some bodily resolution. The unpredictability makes a difference.

Moreover, the felt shift often brings an inner release, even though the external problem about which one is concerned still remains the same. This points up the paradoxical difference between solution and resolution. From a therapeutic point of view, Focusing does not directly solve external problems. What it can do, however, is support change in *your body's way of carrying those problems*.

One workshop participant put it well by saying: "What I'm Focusing on may be painful, but it always feels good when the right symbol comes that fits my felt sense." The content may cause distress, but the moving forward of felt meaning, the resolution in bodily knowing, always brings release.

This method is not without practical implications for problem solving as well. Whenever a felt sense is blocked and unable to flow forward, stress builds up within a person. This stress siphons away energy and attention from the practical tasks at hand. Concentration diminishes; so does the capacity for accurate judgment. Focusing frees a person's resources so he or she can deal more effectively with the practical decisions involved in problem solving.

When a blockage can unfold, when the inner story can be told, tremendous reserves of energy and attention are made available for other pursuits. Blockage, you know, isn't something that happens *to* us. *We hold ourselves in a blocked state,* just as we screw up our faces and hold ourselves tight in the rain. Blocking is something we do to ourselves without really wanting to or in any way knowing how to stop. Yet when we are gifted to break this cycle and let down our defenses, all the energy that went into being uptight is now released.

What usually happens then is that we see things more clearly. We're able to assess problems more objectively, and make more accurate judgments. We don't miss the important things which often slip by when there's static inside from the burden of stress that we carry. We become more alert; and this is always a better way to be when trying to solve practical problems.

Carl Rogers once noted that the most accurate scientific instrument available on this planet is the human organism functioning non-defensively in the presence of a problem. Whenever blockage obstructs the forward flow of personhood, there is a corresponding diminishment in our ability to reason and control. So, we find here a very pragmatic reason for regularly putting down the reins. Sometimes we need to lose our lives in order to find them.

When symbol and felt sense come together within the felt shift of bodily knowing, this marks the completion of a single phase in Focusing. Some people stop at this point if resolution has occurred. But most will want to go on further, sensing that this first step is not enough.

The focuser then begins to work with the symbol that felt right and brought a shift. Is it OK to be with this symbol and the new felt sense that accompanied its arrival? If so, a person can move right into Step #4, allowing oneself to be in the feeling of this newness, permitting it gradually to express itself with an additional appropriate symbol. This cycle can be repeated again and again until a natural stopping point is reached.

For example, if you have been Focusing on a vague sense of displeasure at some project of yours which went awry, perhaps the symbol that eventually comes will have something to do with embarrassment. You didn't measure up. You looked bad in the eyes of your friends. That may be true, but something in you still feels that this doesn't quite say it all. You need to go further. So, if its OK, sit quietly with the felt sense of all that embarrassment, allowing it an opportunity to say what it is. Maybe, after a while, what will come is something about *anger with yourself*. Perhaps that feels more refined, more on target. You're getting closer. If that seems to go far enough, stop. But if you sense that your anger needs to express itself further, then check to see if it would be all right to spend time with this felt sense for a while. Where might it lead you? What tale can it tell in the further unfolding of yourself?

Remember that each time a beginner in Focusing decides to go further, he or she should first check to see whether it's OK to go with this new felt sense. If so, just be in it until it eventually expresses itself with some new symbol.

You might think of this inner process as a chain. Each link which completes one cycle serves as a point of connection and starting point for the next. Perhaps imagining an onion coming apart one layer at a time will help you picture this process.

It's good to point out, as Gendlin does, that no single shift in the felt sense is an absolute answer to anything. Each individual movement must always be situated within a broader pattern.

In focusing you will often find that some words, which come with a strong sense of righteousness at a given moment and give you a body shift, are later

superseded by what comes at a later step. You cannot—and should not—trust any *single* set of words,
any *one* feeling, any *one* body message that comes.
But you can definitely trust the whole series of steps
by which your body moves to resolve and change a
wrong state of being. You can trust that, even if the
words and understanding of a given step are superseded, that step was the right step to come then, at
that moment, and will lead to the right next step
from there.[2]

Trust the overall pattern, therefore. The message is the
process and the process is the message.

This very gentle, non-manipulative procedure is
what Focusing is all about. There are variations, some of
which were developed by colleagues of Dr. Gendlin. There
are instructions about what to do if one gets stuck or can't
get hold of a felt sense. Many strategies are suggested for
maintaining contact with felt meaning as well as what to
do if it should slip away and be lost. All this is fine and
helpful insofar as learning *a technique* is concerned.

But the challenging bio-spiritual dimension of this
experience is that *no matter how carefully one follows any
of these directions, their exact observance can in no way
make something happen!* They are powerless to *effect* the
very change toward which Focusing is aimed. This is the
surprise and challenge one experiences after Focusing
over a period of time.

Careful adherence to the instructions for Focusing
does not *make* anything happen. All it can do is insure
that a person will be more or less situated within the
realm of inner experiencing where change *can* and *may*
occur. It *positions us* for the possibility of bodily resolution. But if there is to be transformation of any sort, *a
radically different, non-voluntary and apparently gratui-
tous element must then take over.* This subtle new dynamic seeks its own direction, measures its own rhythm,
and flows totally beyond the voluntary process which

brought the focuser to the initial point of contact in the first place.

Following the directions for Focusing is much like paddling a canoe from some protected inlet out into the middle of a river. Once there, several things can happen. Sometimes you paddle deliberately into a current. Sometimes, the flow of the river catches you unaware, bearing you along in its grasp. Sometimes you just paddle around and go nowhere. Nothing happens. Following the instructions can only get you out into the middle of your own inner stream. Once there, you soon discover that the stream has a life and movement of its own. *It does not bend to your paddling any more than your canoe can change the course of the river's flow.* All you can do is go with it in case it should catch you and carry you along.

The bio-spiritual challenge involves a delicate balance between purposeful striving and then letting go of the reins. It is a matter of knowing where to be, and then being there with an attitude of patient expectation. It calls for disciplined preparation, but then *allowing* time and space for a deeper knowing and a process to manifest itself.

Focusing supports this bio-spiritual perspective. There lies within each of us a surprise of grace that can arrive within bodily knowing. There is an inner movement beyond all control whose remote horizon seems to be well beyond the passing concerns of everyday survival.

A cosmic story unfolds in each of us. Couched in the language of bodily knowing, it passes largely unnoticed beneath the stream of daily awareness. It conveys a deeper message shrouded in this still early dawn of consciousness evolution. We are as yet only dimly aware of ourselves—each is a flickering point of brightness that fades off into regions of darker unknowing.

Chapter 3

Why we teach Focusing in the context of spirituality

Sometimes we hear the comment that Focusing is primarily a therapeutic tool best used to get one's house in order as a preparation for meditation and spiritual searching. We wish to share our reservations about this view because we in no way limit Focusing to this more obvious therapeutic role.

Focusing, we believe, is far more integrative and comprehensive in its psychological dynamics. In one simple experience it unites the benefits of psycho-physical therapy with meditation's emphasis on centering, active receptivity, and expanded awareness. Moreover, all this is realized in a personally tailored, developmental fashion according to the rhythm and ability of each person to integrate this step into their lives. We see no reason to limit Focusing to problem solving, crisis intervention, or just the preparation for meditation—although all these uses are certainly valid.

We feel that Focusing offers a developmental approach to some of the most basic elements of meditation. Wherever the focuser happens to be in their spiritual development, he or she is plunged directly into two essential ingredients of meditation: an initial striving, preparatory aspect, and then the alert waiting and receptivity which are so often rewarded with an eventual shift in consciousness.

Focusing teaches a marvelous balance because it integrates these two essential elements of personal and spiritual growth. It can create a posture, a presence, eventually even a lifestyle of "caring detachment" so difficult to realize in our competitive, control-oriented society. The integrative nature of Focusing somehow reconciles the apparent opposites of "caring" and "detachment" into a higher level synthesis within the focuser. This synthesis manifests itself most profoundly in the maturing quality of presence with which one can live one's ordinary life.

In this chapter we would like to show how Focusing can address three critical issues in spirituality.

1. The perennial problem of "getting out of the mind"
2. The challenge of being drawn into an awareness of some Larger Process
3. How one's own "body knowing" is a key to forward movement in these two areas

What do we mean by *mind?* The word is used in many ways within different spiritual traditions. We use it here in a limited sense that refers to the rational, linear thinking process. It is a way of identifying all the *chatter in the skull* associated with analyzing, planning, and problem solving.

Our own search for a psychologically healthy spirituality has led both of us to conclude that getting out of the mind is really allowing one's self to be drawn more fully into body knowing. *You get out of the mind by getting into the body*. These are not separate or distinct activities. Moreover, body knowing provides the immediate, practical framework within which spiritual awareness is apparently meant to function.

Human evolution is rooted in an "embodied" person, and "higher level consciousness" involves an unfolding of the entire person. Although such a fundamental realization appears to be part of every wisdom tradition, it is also something that various expressions of this tradition in religion and spirituality have often lost or neglected. This is certainly the case within Christianity today. Realizing that a more holistic, process-oriented, bio-spirituality was needed to support a *felt sense* for having one's being within some greater Mystery, we have been drawn to Focusing.

There are two critical issues in spiritual development as far as we are concerned. The first is to discover an holistic approach for letting go of the mind's omnipotent control as a prelude to allowing some broader wisdom within the entire human organism to speak. The second is to allow the unique next step that is *me* to emerge as an integral, harmonious expression of some Larger Process.

For centuries various spiritual traditions have identified a blocking experience of the mind as *the* central issue in spiritual growth. The problem of seeking to use the finely honed power of reason to control everything in one's life seems to be the primary issue faced by anyone serious about spiritual growth. The omnipotence which we grant to the power of intellect becomes our downfall. This magnificent potential of reason was never meant to be a tool with which to control absolutely everything that touches human existence.

Yet we all balk at the risk involved in setting aside the very means by which we are accustomed to survive. We cherish our ability to "think out" and "solve" problems, and rightfully so. But the tendency to vest so much of our personal identity in an exercise of reason and control can deafen us to the inviting call and surrender to some greater meaning and purpose in life.

One soon discovers at the threshold of spiritual awareness an interwoven web of uniquely personal fears. We are reluctant to let go of the security we create with our wits. We are afraid of losing our more or less familiar self-identity. This is a familiar scenario for any maturing human being, as well as for those engaged in the helping professions and for spiritual counselors.

It is incredible how our ambitions, dreams, hopes, and fears, even our deepest longings for peace and justice can often confuse and sidetrack us from concentrating our attention on this central issue. We find so many sincere, well-intentioned people who continually fall into the trap of living as though ideals could be actualized by better *understanding* them, preaching them, researching or analyzing them, discussing or organizing them into rules and regulations. Some become so involved in this monumental effort that like the king and his mesmerized followers they are unable to see that everyone is naked and things simply are not working. It is a difficult lesson for idealists as well as for generous and dedicated religious activists to learn. Ideals, praiseworthy goals, morals, ethics, religious values, worship—all are just as open to misuse as any so-called worldly pursuit. These, too, can become a hindrance to letting go of the mind's instinctive tendency to control everything.

Whenever someone falls under the spell of using methods of control in order to achieve spiritual ideals or religious goals, such values and altruistic pursuits, praiseworthy in themselves, can become obstacles. They blind a person to the very direction and answers which may be sought within the benevolence and grace of the Cosmos. We have found that Focusing provides a practical framework within which trust can grow. It is a trust which gradually makes possible the actual living of what our ideals represent.

We also find that Focusing can support spiritual growth by inviting a person to step beyond the mind's perennial quest for control. It provides a practical framework for encouraging that "art of allowing" within which we can gently be taught to trust a deeper bodily-felt wisdom. Focusing has an uncanny way of keeping a person on the right track. It constantly surfaces the pivotal, personal issues which provide an immediate point of entry into bodily knowing. By its very nature, therefore, Focusing creates the right climate for spirituality.

While Focusing, one does not introduce any of the more traditional approaches used to gain meditative attention. One sets aside prayerful considerations, the reading of scriptures, using a mantrum, mandala or koan, the Jesus Prayer, one's own breathing, or any other physical action like dance or aikido. These activities do not necessarily center attention on, nor express the unique next step of unfolding that is proper to the one who focuses—so, they are not used.

Rather, Focusing brings attention as well as receptivity to bear on what the focuser allows his or her organism to indicate has first priority in life right now. Something uniquely personal which *feels* like it is important enough to be more fully aware of with one's entire being.

The particular value of Focusing, when used in a spiritual context, lies in the way it opens a door beyond thinking and control. Instead of programmed input or activity that may be used to draw attention beyond the mind, Focusing allows a bodily-felt sense for the next step in life to form and provide the practical framework within which meditative attention is realized. In a single act, the focuser is drawn out of the mind and into the body. But the body side of this equation is one which, as we shall see in a moment, is a potentially fruitful interface between ego's concern for control and an inrush of grace from the Cosmos.

What we have in Focusing, then, is a setting for sound spirituality that is simultaneously realized within a context of sound psychology.

In our culture it is difficult to judge accurately the contribution of religion and the various spiritual disciplines. What elements in them actually contribute to healthy human development and what, instead, cause harm? Trying to sort this out is like stumbling through a booby-trapped field. It's so easy to step into the wrong place and get blown off the path of your own inner wisdom. We can easily be beguiled by the promises and rewards of this or that spiritual path.

People long today as always for personal meaning, security, and connectedness. They seek ethical and moral guidelines for a better understanding of the "why's" and "what's" of life. In an age that is characterized by the absence of such guidelines, people welcome almost any attempt to respond to this vacuum. Such vulnerability, though, gives rise to a naivete and a hiatus in critical perception where few people realize that the way they use religion *is actually part of the problem* of blocked change and growth, not the solution. Entire communities and groups of religious or spiritually oriented people become thwarted in this fashion. They pass on a kind of blindness from generation to generation, all in the name of God, religion, or enlightenment of some kind or other.

Focusing brings a badly needed freshness and honesty into all of this. One of our workshop participants tried to describe something of her experience in a recent letter. She wrote:

> Focusing reaches the inner knowing and bypasses the outer beliefs. The Spirit knows when things are not "right" at the deepest level, when the intellect can only guess at the cause, and not always accurately, most times preventing those "felt shifts" wherein the real cause starts to dissipate. It is healing from the inside-out, affording the human mind little chance for self-deception.

Another person wrote:

> There can be so much self-deception in a talking to God kind of prayer. Focusing, though, helps me to put my body and all that's there (hurting, scary, or otherwise) where my good intentions are in prayer. I can't use talking to God as an escape from being in touch with the truth of myself. One must let go of the controlling mind and all its chatter, let go into what

the body knows. Otherwise, you can't focus. It puts
my trust in God, my faith in Divine Providence right
on the line! I have to risk letting the answers come
as they will, not make them up myself. Focusing invites me *actually to believe with my body*, not just my
mind. It invites me to live my faith in a benevolent,
loving Providence as a whole person.

Statements such as these reveal the journey inward.
They come like letters from a distant traveller walking
some risky byway beyond the mind's control. A good nov-
elist or biographer can never really catch the meanings,
the deeper dimensions, or connectedness of people's lives
without somehow "getting inside" the skin of his or her
subject. So too, each of us is meant to be drawn inside to
touch the marvelous, unique story that is ourselves.

The psychological dynamics of Focusing encourage
us to *allow symbols to happen*. Such symbols can teach
us to wait patiently before the awesome Mystery of humankind, a mystery hidden within the story in our own
bodies. Being on the right path to discover this message
seems to hinge on whether we learn to allow that story of
The Whole which is in us, to appear. When the symbol
comes unbidden, when the surprise of a new direction unfolds within our bodily knowing, we realize what it is to
be drawn beyond the mind. We also sense at the same
time a benevolent process which carries us beyond our
limited, control-oriented selves.

There is a story in time and human history unfolding
in each of us. It is a story with roots, a cosmic tied-in-ness
and pattern of meaning not bounded by the limitations of
our particular moment in history. But to open even the
first chapter, let alone continue reading until the glimmer
of some Larger Pattern and rootedness begin to emerge,
involves getting inside our bodies in a special way. This,
it seems, is the key message contained within the perennial spiritual traditions of the world. And this is where
we feel Focusing can make an exciting and significant
contribution.

The Kingdom of Heaven is within! Our individual stories, which are integral to the entire Cosmic narrative, are written in our bodies. Any approach to spirituality which neglects or tries to bypass this blunt bio-spiritual fact is ultimately dead-ended and off the track of human evolution.

Some people write today about having "recovered their bodies and feelings" as though this were an accomplished fact and now they can go on to something else. Others strive through "spiritual" practices to transcend both body and feelings. The two of us believe that the story we are meant to write with our lives is one that continues to unfold, but not within some disembodied center of awareness. It blossoms forth within a bodily-felt sense that *is* consciousness-potential itself.

"Recovering our bodies" is really the lifelong process of allowing the knowing-potential of the entire organism to open, thereby revealing an underlying plot of unity hidden between the lines of what appears as a disconnected narrative. Whenever a felt sense unfolds, whenever a symbol appears from beyond the narrowed edge of reason and control, then we can catch sight of the Larger Mystery written within the story that is ourselves. We can begin to trust. Perhaps more important, we may discover a gifted believing that is written in our bodies.

Each experience of *felt shift* opens an extraordinary window on a vast, largely unexplored world of human awareness. It is a realm of tangible *connection*. A place from which to touch and taste with bodily knowing. Beyond every rationalization and mental construct, here at last one finds the body's inward lookout point on an expanding universe.

Given the cultural heritage of most Westerners today, we believe Focusing has a potential for becoming, perhaps, the most important ingredient in a lifestyle which we would call spiritual. Spiritual, in the sense that this mode of self-awareness called Focusing provides a structure within which one can bring the consciousness potential of the whole organism within the scope of some Larger Cosmic Process.

Chapter 4

Humor, Playfulness, and surprise

The vulnerability of ego

Focusing is full of surprises, and the unexpected occurs quite often. One session in particular stands out for the two of us. Ed had experienced a painful, somewhat foreboding felt sense. It was quite uncomfortable for him. Together we tried various approaches, hoping the right symbol might break through to awareness; but all to no avail. The effort seemed futile until suddenly Ed had a tremendous urge to giggle. It was an infectious inner tickling that could not be contained. We both found it a relief to laugh, and we shared our amusement at something neither of us could fully comprehend. Then, in the midst of this hilarity, the dark cloud of a felt sense suddenly poked its head around some inner psychic corner and shouted, "Boo!" Immediately and spontaneously the image of a laughing Buddha appeared; it was seated in a lotus position with hands raised in the air merrily laughing.

At this point there was a distinct felt shift. The inner landscape became totally transformed. The felt sense was entirely different. Yet the foreboding aspect of inner meaning had not been symbolized as we had expected. Nevertheless, despite its initial, somewhat ominous expression, the inner felt sense was now no longer an enemy. A kind of gentle amusement, even playfulness, appeared once the felt sense had been owned and accepted.

The flavor of this experience remained for several days. It was totally unexpected, and we enjoyed talking about its implications. More than anything else, the spontaneous upsurge of humor and lightheartedness piqued our curiosity. We were charmed by the element of surprise.

There is a comfortable predictability about reason. Maybe that's why it has never been thought of as the royal road of spiritual advancement. Reason can never comprehend the miraculous, the unpredictable, the larger pattern. In the narrowed world of control there is little room for playfulness and surprise. Indeed, surprise is the enemy! *Yet availability for surprise is a necessary disposition for growth in the spiritual life.*

An example of just such a surprise came during one of Pete's Focusing sessions a few years ago. We'll keep our narrative in the first person to preserve the flavor of this unique experience. Pete's story unfolds as follows:

> It was a distressing time for me. A recurring bout of severe lower back spasms associated with a cracked vertebra had kept me in bed for over a week. Along with the physical pain, I was also trying to cope with mounting fear and depression. Catastrophic expectations loomed large in my awareness as I chafed at my immobility and the unpredictable nature of what I was experiencing. How soon might this happen again? How long would it last? The slightest twinge of pain pushed me toward preoccupation with self and defensive isolation. Presence to anything other than my own panic and concern was practically impossible.
>
> Talking to myself did no good. Praying was hopeless. No amount of reasoning was able to break

through my brooding sense of fear and depression. It just wouldn't let go! I felt divided against myself. All of me that wanted to live and move with ease and freedom felt squeezed into the upper part of my head and shoulders, as though trying to shrink as far away as possible from the pain in my lower back.

I desperately wanted direction in all of this confusion. I not only wanted meaning, but also some way of *growing through* rather than simply *enduring* this experience. I needed to be in my pain and my frustrated feeling of dependence in a different way. So I used Focusing to draw near to all my depression, helplessness, and the terrifying possibilities I had conjured up for myself. Instead of seeking a direction from *outside* my fear, I finally decided to walk the inner road to see what might happen.

The image which eventually came surprised me. It was far more profound than I realized at first. It was a response that answered my problem by restating the question. There was a distinct body sense to the imagery. It felt right.

A new perspective was born. The image helped me walk *through* pain to a broadened vista on life and myself. It was as though I could actually feel myself being drawn to some larger picture. The knowing which I experienced in that brief moment was a realizing of the way *through* my fear and confusion. *That in itself was the answer!* Not an answer *to* fear, but a way of being *in* fear or any feeling, positive or negative, which might allow the unveiling of some deeper bio-spiritual perspective.

The image came in a flash, from the midst of pain and confusion. It came unbidden with no prior consideration on my part. It was the memory of an incident I had not recalled for almost forty years. A trivial event. Yet, now it returned with meaning and a power that caught me by surprise. It made a connection! And in that connection I was blessed with the first of a long series of bodily-felt releases from fear and tension. What, then, was the image?

As a youngster I had, for health reasons, attended a boarding school in the Arizona desert. It was an isolated little ranch about twenty miles from Tucson. Horseback riding was available, and I soon fell in love with getting out on a mount and riding for miles through the desert.

We weren't allowed to do this alone, of course. But one morning at dawn, when I was only seven years old, I used the watering trough to stand on and saddled up alone before any staff or children were stirring. Then I rode straight out into the sunrise. It was a glorious day and I explored the desert for an hour or more, giving little thought to anything except what lay ahead of me. At some point it dawned on me to get my bearings, and I turned to check for familiar landmarks. But the surrounding arroyos gave no hint of a direction home. There were no familiar markers. No paths or trails. Just sagebrush, cactus, and an unending series of little hills that all looked the same. I realized with a sudden chill that I was lost!

Searching for a while, I desperately tried to find my way home, but I soon realized it was hopeless. I remember my inner panic and growing sense of isolation—much like feelings that would come in later life whenever fear or confusion would overtake me. Only gradually did my attention return to my horse, who was peacefully waiting for me to signal with reins and stirrups where we were to go next.

At that point I was inspired to do one of the few sensible things a youngster in my predicament could do. I stopped trying to figure things out for myself and made what may have been one of the first consciously deliberate acts of trust in my young life. I knew I was lost, but deep down I felt that *the horse knew his way home!* The remembered experience of how I deliberately lifted the reins and let them drop on the horse's neck somehow fit what my body knew about pain and confusion as I focused forty years later. It had not been forgotten!

There had been a deliberate letting go and trusting out there in the desert years before. It was a letting go of everything that wanted to control the situation, a kind of abandonment to some wisdom that lay beyond anything I could muster within myself.

That morning among the sage brush and cacti, the horse's first response to my loosening of the reins was to begin nibbling the sparse grass at his feet. I didn't urge him anywhere but just left the reins loose and waited. Unaccustomed to such lack of direction, he stood still for a while looking about before he moved to get more grass.

I recall wondering how long it would take him to get the point. I didn't know my way back to the ranch and had no way of communicating this to the horse. It would take time for him to realize that I had voluntarily become a bundle of inert baggage which he could carry anywhere he wished.

I remember how hard it was to resist the temptation to move him about. I desperately wanted to reassert my control, holding the reins, guiding him now one way, now another. But my feeling, even as a child, was that he had to experience a sense of himself as boss if we were ever to get home before nightfall. And so I waited . . . and waited . . . and waited. It seemed endless.

Finally I noticed the horse stretching his neck, shaking his head, and testing the looseness of the reins. Instead of grazing haphazardly, he began to move in a definite direction. Snatching mouthfuls of grass, he would move on a few paces before reaching for another tuft as we passed.

Gradually the stops became less frequent, his pace quickened, and eventually he broke into a trot, with only occasional questioning looks over his shoulder, and then a determined, careening gallop. Ahead lay oats, the corral, and getting this infernal saddle off his back—not to mention the young rider hanging on for dear life.

It was a wild ride home; I narrowly missed the outstretched spines of cholla cactus and barely grazed the giant saguaro so plentiful in that part of the desert. Terrified, I clutched the saddle horn, torn between a desperate desire to rein in this lurching juggernaut and the equally strong fear that if I did we might never get home.

Finally familiar landmarks appeared. We slowed, stopped, and rested a bit. I even imagined a mischievous glint in the equine eye as he turned to see how I was doing.

The rest of the return was uneventful. Little did I then realize that the personal significance of this event would lie dormant in me for almost forty years before coming back to teach me more about myself.

I have learned through Focusing that the way home is written deep within each of us. Somewhere beneath all of our daily *reacting*—getting jobs done, meals prepared, bills paid, and all our survival planning—lies a realm of deeper meaning, purpose, and direction. The horse, as I have found through Focusing, is really a largely unowned aspect of ourselves. There is something within each of us that knows the real meaning of human life. At certain times it can break through the shallow awareness that fills most of our waking moments.

What I want to say is that during the Focusing episode I am presently describing, my pain, fear, depression, and helplessness in that instant came to be for me like the horse. Instead of seeking to ride these feelings in a controlling way, I realized what was needed was for me to be with/in them in a different manner.

When I hold the reins, it *feels differently* than when I let them fall. I'm speaking not only physically but psychologically. When you are in control, everything comes to you as to a spider at the center of its web. Control means readiness to react. Being on top of the survival game.

Letting go of the reins is more like *being carried*. It is a different psychological stance, a different physical feeling. Your center somehow changes; it becomes less precise and broader in scope. It *includes* more! You feel and respond out of something bigger than your ability to control.

That, for me, is the beginning of bio-spiritual awareness! It is finding a way through to some larger *At Homeness* written deep within bodily knowing. There is wisdom in the horse, and the horse is *us!*

I believe this is why that image from childhood means so much to me. It helped me to realize that fear and helplessness are a special doorway into a more profound realm of what my life is all about. I found an encouraging sign that I was on the right track.

I didn't gain control over fear. Rather, I discovered a bodily-felt way of being in fear so it could draw me into the mystery of some farther horizon. I didn't *solve* problems so much as *gain a new perspective*. The surprising thing, though, was how that change of perspective affected my body! I could *feel* the tightness of fear begin to unbend. Yet I had no control over what was happening. I was not *doing* something. It was doing itself!

There is so much mystery in bodily knowing. It doesn't follow the dictates of reason. One finds, instead, a world of wisdom and surprise that can only be entered in a very special way. As the cowboys of old had to check their guns at the barroom door, we too must first lay down the overriding need to control all of our lives before we cross the threshold of bio-spiritual journeying.

Each of us must learn our own personal language of transcendence. There is a difference between *solutions* which we think out in our minds, and a gifted *resolution* in a way our bodies carry issues and problems. Playfulness and surprise often accompany this graced inner release. We are drawn beyond the narrow scope of reason into some greater sense for ourselves. There is vastness within. There is a vital cosmic connection which lies on the edge of human awareness.

Just writing these words, now, calls up a felt sense.

The reserve of bodily knowing rushes in to say "Yes" in its own inimitable fashion.

We recall a short vacation we had in Montreal during the World's Fair—Expo '67. It was a day of sharp contrasts as we visited the Soviet and British pavilions one right after the other. A certain heaviness hung over the Russian exhibit with its excessive emphasis on productivity. The goal of several Five Year Plans had either been achieved or surpassed. Technical competence and achievements in space—all were there and were of great importance to the Soviets. One could not help being impressed. Yet after a time it became tiring.

Outside the pavilion the sun was shining as we strolled over to the next exhibit. What a surprise! Upon entering the British pavilion we were led through a series of clever exhibits in which the English poked gentle fun at their own foibles and idiosyncrasies, as only the British can do. It was a delightful journey that brought a refreshing inner lightness. Toward the end we were led through a twisting, tunnel-like enclosure which abruptly opened out to a large room filled with immense El Greco-like figures by Giacometti, their arms extended skyward. The experience brought goose pimples. There was a sense of movement, a breadth of vision. The long sweep of transcendence had burst forth like a natural conclusion to the humor and playfulness which preceded it. Everything was so right! It fit. It hung together, and we felt we were at the edge of something very great.

We walked beneath these towering figures for a bit, like miniature wanderers through a gigantic frozen ballet. And then we left. But the memory has remained, and it returns now like some forgotten melody to add a richer texture to the current unfolding of our lives.

Humor and playfulness are somehow part of transcendence. They are one more way the human person says "Yes" to being within some greater reality. They are an unrationalized, organismic admission that the limited center and sense of self are *not* the total picture. In such experiences one catches a glimpse of growing comfortableness with going beyond the familiar, the habitual, and the structure-bound. It's OK to have limitations, not to know all the answers, not to have everything under control.

Focusing opens the possibility for such surprises within bodily knowing. It reveals inner movements much like a mountain stream than keeps on inviting you around some enchanting next bend.

But there is a darker side to all this as well, an unsettling reluctance to face the nightmare. *Resistance!* This, too, colors our experience of transcendence. There is humor, lightness, challenge, and surprise. But there is also the reluctance to take the next step.

Let's consider the disquieting nature of this bio-spiritual journey. What perceived risks cause us to hesitate? Why do we so often feel an inner tensing at what this venture may demand from us? Can we, perhaps, find direction for ourselves right within the reluctant foot-dragging which frequently characterizes our first halting steps into this realm of bodily knowing?

There is an unsettling dimension to the bio-spiritual enterprise. We inevitably hesitate at the start, hanging back from the risks of this hazardous venture. We resist letting go into organismic awareness not only because reason protests that it is often unreliable. There is also the far more disturbing call to step beyond the very familiarity of reason itself!

Unreliability we can somehow cope with. It's the vulnerability we cannot stand! Letting go into a felt sense means letting go of reason's control.

Spiritual teachers as well as the wisdom literature of many religious traditions have all explored this hanging back from taking the next step. Such resistance, though, is actually a blessing in disguise because it teaches us so much about ourselves. It is never in itself a block to bio-spiritual progress! Like the nightmare, it can be a marvelous teacher, a wonderful guide, an avenue of entry into the miraculous.

The term *ego* is often used in this context. Like other words it has many meanings. The two of us are not interested in listing these meanings here. We would like, however, to share what this word has come to mean for us. We identify *ego* as the entire experience associated with trying to be in control. All our survival efforts, the activity of reason, our identity associated with this manner of knowing—all this, for us, is ego.

Hopefully, you can conclude from this that ego is never something to be gotten rid of. Without it you couldn't survive. Yet it needs to be located properly in the broader framework of a more complete human life. As in Focusing, there are times for deliberate effort, for paddling your canoe. Then there are times for setting such striving aside. But even when doing this, ego is never completely abandoned. The bud is always in the flower, but the flower is always *more than* the bud. At this point one simply waits to be called farther forward, if that is to happen. It is a moment of potentially tangible transcendence. It is being touched by grace.

You might think of the caterpillar; how busy it is. With a magnifying glass you can be amazed by the spectacle of its survival activity as the caterpillar chews a path along the edge of a luscious leaf. You behold the dynamic synthesis of organic matter into organic matter. There is a deliberate, sometimes frenzied effort to gorge as much food as possible into this little creature.

But then comes the slowing down, a quieting, a period of greater attending within. Now deeper forces take over. No longer the passionate quest for gratification. Instead, a cocoon of stillness. Then it happens. Metamorphosis!

Ego is like the caterpillar. An exciting place of beginning and transformation. It is an apt image of our Body of Flesh within which, one day, there can arise a magnificent dawning of Spirit.

But what of our own metamorphosis? Where can we begin? Perhaps, like the Senoi child in a dream, we will discover the deeper place of Spirit by starting with our own nightmare—the current resistance which holds us back from further unfolding.

It's interesting and instructive to discover the various patterns of ego defense a person may build up against getting more involved with their bodily knowing. Sometimes these defenses are subtle and can be quite funny. Pete, for example, used to find when beginning to Focus that he was confronted almost immediately by the same recurring theme. After only a moment of trying to be in the felt sense, an identical pattern of resistance would appear. *It was the list of jobs he still had to do around the house and in the office!* Again and again this list would appear and Pete would be led into considering the various items it contained, planning which of them he would do next, what tools were needed, what purchases had to be made, and so on.

In the beginning we thought of the list as a major distraction and its regular appearance was greeted with considerable annoyance. But before long the real significance became obvious. During one Focusing session Ed made the suggestion: "How does always having this list of things to do feel in your body right now? Why not just focus on that?" The suggestion was not meant to get Pete involved with thinking *about* the various items on this list. Rather, he was simply invited to attend more carefully to the inner sense of this image, allowing the feeling of it to unfold.

This particular Focusing episode led the two of us on a long and interesting journey. We got into many things, primarily the need we have for control and the fear of losing control. We journeyed together through the intense satisfaction that comes from getting jobs done. Crossing things off the list! We then sat with the anxiety of situations where tasks never seemed to be completed, where there were too many loose ends. In each instance what we touched was not the unique content of some item that could be thought about. Rather, it was an opportunity to *be in* the unfinishedness of the task, the loss of control, the good feeling of completing a project, and the felt meaning of all this.

In an amazing way, this initial resistance proved to be the best possible avenue of entry into the Focusing process. The experience has been repeated again and again in workshops and counseling sessions with others. The resistance which most severely blocks letting go into bodily knowing provides a priceless point of entry into the further story of felt meaning within each of us. No matter what the resistance—fatigue, being overwhelmed by it all, a sense that all this is silly, terror at what might be discovered, feeling embarrassed, not wanting to take up so much of other people's time, feeling uncomfortable because I can't find any problem to focus on, feeling blank and at an inner standstill, being bored—all these resistances and many more have turned into valuable doorways and marvelous beginnings.

Any hanging back from your painful felt sense is *always* a sign of hope! If this seems strange, remember that right within the resistance itself you can discover another loose thread leading into the tapestry of bodily knowing. Whenever pain is too much to bear, whenever knocking at the front door of a troublesome felt sense requires more courage than you can muster, there is always a side entrance, a cellar window, some unnoticed opening through which to gain entry.

Recall Step #3 in the Focusing process, checking whether it's OK to be with a felt sense. When the answer is "No," this does not mean everything comes to a crashing halt. You have an alternative. Instead of taking your difficult felt sense head on, you ask whether it would be all right to spend time with the repugnance, fear, or apprehension that lies behind your "No." You turn *to the resistance itself* as your next best opening into what needs to be focused upon.

Hope, then, lies in the very hanging back through which you shun involvement with bodily knowing. There is a feeling edge in such resistance. It is real. Tangible. Accessible. An alternate path along which to be drawn toward your next forward step. It's not always easy. But neither does it leave you hopelessly mired in the dead end of your own depression and discouragement. There is never any circumstance within which you can't find some doorway of growth.

We frequently wonder about this apparent paradox. Why does inner resistance and defensiveness so often provide the best port of entry into bodily knowing? Why should nightmares pave a way toward the birth of some new inner creation? It's so strange. Mysterious. Teilhard de Chardin closed his epic work, *The Phenomenon of Man*, with this searching final reflection: "In one manner or the other it still remains true that, even in the view of the mere biologist, the human epic resembles nothing so much as a way of the Cross."

Survival means strengthening the ego and extending the refinement of control. Evolution, on the other hand, means gambling all on the possibility of being drawn farther forward in the unfolding of our own story. Crucifixion lies not in the goal toward which we are carried. That is a joy. A bodily resurrection! It's in the *letting go* of security associated with what we already know that is so painful. That's what we feel in such resistance. It is the challenge of believing. We must first mature beyond ego-perception before we are drawn into the unfolding of a more integral and lasting Self.

Survival, of course, is absolutely necessary if evolution is to succeed. But the perspective of ego is so narrow. It lacks depth; human depth. The approach to everything is so limited. Always seeing from the outside. Calculating. Manipulating. Predicting. Controlling. What needs to be abandoned are not these fine survival skills but the sense for ourselves which has become totally identified with this narrower perspective.

But how can this occur? Is it something we deliberately *do* for ourselves—setting out to divest ourselves of ego? The two of us don't think so.

Michael Murphy once wrote a marvelously speculative story about an enthralling experiment on the leading edge of human evolution. It includes intriguing references to Einstein-Rosen bridges, mind-holes, DNA molecules, and passages to other worlds. The principal character in this fascinating enterprise is a young man whose name provides the title for the book, *Jacob Atabet*.[2] Jacob attempts to journey into the farther reaches of human consciousness. Expanding awareness into both microcosm and macrocosm is the goal of his heroic adventure.

Jacob Atabet is consumed by a burning desire to discover how individual awareness can ultimately break through to cosmic consciousness. How can a person transcend the limitations of ego and the individual sensory world? For Jacob, the question is simple enough: Is it possible to change the rules of what he calls "the body game?"

In his pursuit of an answer, Jacob seeks a hidden formula through which by personal effort he may transcend the limits of reason and ego-awareness. Practicing what he regards as an evolutionary asceticism, he strives by sheer acts of the will to reach beyond the limited knowing potential of his own organism into the embrace of some wider consciousness. In the end, Jacob Atabet nearly destroys himself, finally realizing that there are no shortcuts.

Michael Murphy's story recounts a fictional attempt to reach past the boundaries of ego. In order for this to happen there must be changes in the rules of the body-game. *But can we make such changes by ourselves?*

We think not. Effort there must be, but effort of a different sort. Not a straining to evolve, but a constant, disciplined faithfulness to our own advancing story. We do not change the rules. *The rules are changed for us!*

Jacob Atabet, we feel, tragically missed the mark. Being drawn beyond ego is not something that is wrested from the universe like some prized mineral that is arduously dug from the earth. Rather, *it is given to us* as butterfly wings emerge from the caterpillar when the time is ripe.

The question of ego-transcendence, then, is not some esoteric adventure, a striving to achieve an altered state of consciousness. Neither is it an asceticism of willpower and control. True enlightenment appears to be nothing more *nor less* than taking your own next step, *allowing* a process to go forward.

The fruits of successful Focusing are never grunted up by personal effort. You cannot deliberately set out to change something through Focusing. The change is gift. Grace. The inner struggle is not one of will power, trying to *make something happen*. Rather, the effort involved is in remaining faithful to your own deeper story, believing in the *depth* of yourself. Taking up the daily cross of being in each resistance which holds you back from letting go into your next step forward.

The prophet Isaiah records a powerful and compelling image for the Hebrew people. In it the God of Israel speaks a message which echoes down through the centuries. It brings strength and guidance to many people who follow the Judaeo-Christian path.

> When you pass through the waters
>   I will be with you;
> when you walk through fire
>   you shall not be burned,
> and the flame shall not consume you.
>   (*Isa. 43:2 RSV*)

An enduring Presence animates the history and the wandering of those who have been nourished by this Old Testament tradition.

But apply these words of the prophet to your own inner world. There is a remarkable parallel with the unfolding of inner life. The felt sense can be a place of fire and flood, confusion, turbulence, and pain. It is beyond control, beyond the crafted security that ego can provide.

A call into the desert drew the Hebrews from their familiar Egyptian landscape into the untamed wilderness of Sinai. What they lived as an external, historical event we experience today in the unfolding of our own inner sense of self. Focusing provides an Exodus context for each of us. It places us in the wilderness area of our own open-ended journey, our pilgrimage, our wandering in the realm of evolutionary surprise.

This is a desert place for most of us because we usually come to know ourselves as ego, as the ones who strive for control. Yet here, control must be abandoned in favor of a new way of being.

Two vital experiences happened to the Israelites during their Exodus wandering, two experiences that radically transformed their sense of themselves. They discovered a new identity for themselves, and in it they were touched by the saving power of God.

The desert was beyond all control, yet out of this strange wilderness came wonders and surprise. Water gushed forth from a rock. Manna fell from above. They were given a cloud by day and a pillar of fire by night to guide them.

The Israelites heard a voice which spoke to them in this wilderness, a voice from beyond the habitual, the familiar, the secure. The protective shell of their hardened ego was blistered by the desert sun; cracked; broken; eventually transformed. Exodus for the Israelites was a time of conversion. Beyond all their resistance a new identity lay waiting to be born. They were to discover themselves as gift, as graced. They would find within the limitations of their own flesh the seed of God.

So, too, with each one of us in our time. What Hebrew could imagine the surprise of living water gushing forth from an arid desert rock? Who among us can imagine that the hard place of inner resistance—anger, frustration, fear, and confusion—might one day open up to point the way home?

Do we yet know the gift that we are? Have we explored that inner reserve beyond our ego?

Exodus is now. It is the story of Everyman, Everywoman, and Everychild. It is a journey lived over and over again. It is the commitment to a greater depth of humanness. It is finding in life much more than simply the will to survive. It is testing the waters of deeper identity. Being drawn beyond all willing into the embrace of a wider bio-spiritual quest.

Chapter 5

Restoring inner process

The evolution
of God consciousness

Have you ever experienced moments of quiet in which you suddenly realized your life has become little more than a series of *reactions* to one crisis after another? As each of us grows older, we long to live more of each remaining day not like a cork bobbing up and down on the waves of other people's events. Rather, we feel a compelling need to discover unfolding direction *from within*. *My* life. *My* reason for being. *My* unique story.

The storyteller's art has always been more than simply knowing how to communicate information. It is the gift of keeping a tale alive, ever moving, always unfolding with unexpected twists and turns that delight both the reader and the listener.

So too when men and women seek the meaning of their lives, they look for more than information about themselves. Beneath this search is a profound desire to experience an inner *unfolding* of their own personal stories. They want to experience *forward movement* that is uniquely their own. Not something programmed from outside, but an expression arising from deep within themselves.

An underlying instinct for a broader spiritual horizon animates this irrepressible longing. There is an opening *within the flow of ourselves,* an inner window through which the rising sun of a new creation can warm the next phase of evolution. It is sustained by fleeting glimpses into what human beings are in the process of becoming.

This is not some vision of where we can arrive and what we might achieve through personal effort. Rather, it is an unfolding, not of our making, that moves toward destinations beyond human comprehension. It has a different tempo and rhythm that beats beneath the ordered security we all program into our lives.

But we must come to know this transformation, learning the subtle signs which unfold this vast cosmic drama. There is a territory to be trodden within ourselves; it is to be observed, cultivated, and lived with through our personal seasons of joy, sorrow, expectation, passion, and gratification. We must each follow the thread of our own unique stories. We must wind along with them to find in the unfolding a rootedness in something greater than ourselves.

But where can we look within everyday experience for an entryway into such a surprise?

In our quest for an answer, let's look once again at those hurts and the blockage that for many people so rarely unfolds. A critical item that caught Eugene Gendlin's attention as a therapist was not the *content* of personal problems, but the *body's knowing or carrying* of those problems.

That's an important distinction! It identifies a privileged doorway through which the bio-spiritual can eventually appear.

From a therapeutic point of view, *how* a person carries a difficulty is often far more important than the *content* that is carried. Gendlin and other psychologists have noted that successful therapy involves more than a client's simply learning something new about himself or herself. Rather, success emerges from a distinct *physical shift* in the bodily sense of a problem or a life situation. A *felt shift* to use Gendlin's more technical phrase.

Dr. Gendlin observed with many people that although the content with which they worked might be painful, getting the correct symbol together with their felt sense always felt right and good. The problem was not necessarily solved, but the way that it was *carried* could be changed.

We received a touching illustration of this fact in a recent letter from one of our workshop participants.

> Enclosed is the announcement of the birth of my son. Unfortunately, I was not able to have a natural childbirth as Jeremy went into fetal distress—so, I was put "under" and he was out within five minutes. So much for a drugless birth. He was a very sick baby— he had a blood transfusion in the first twenty-four hours, and oxygen for five days and finally he came home after twelve days in intensive care.
>
> I am thankful that I attended the weekend of learning how to focus—as it helped me deal with what has happened.
>
> Before I found out that he was a Down's Syndrome baby, I first was *very* upset at not experiencing any part of the birth—I felt so empty at having a life inside of me and then waking up with it gone—not even beside me. In fact, the situation of his birth is more difficult for me than having a handicapped child.
>
> Using the focusing has helped me accept the situation of his birth and condition and not dwell on the "Why me?" question. I learned the important thing— that I love him, and God gave me a very special child.
>
> In fact, I feel lucky because my life now has a specific direction—to help Jeremy develop to the best of his potential.

> There are still many difficult moments, but with the help of prayer, focusing, relatives, friends and other Down's Syndrome parents it makes it a lot easier.
>
> Someday, I hope to return for a follow-up. Thank you again for teaching me.

Perhaps you know from personal experience what it means to be suddenly gifted with purpose and direction in your life. It may not always be what you would have chosen for yourself. Yet the unexpected arrival of such meaning can release enormous reserves of energy and, in some instances, lifelong commitment. Such an experience rarely provides a *solution* to the practical, sometimes tragic difficulties you may confront. But sitting down with a tragedy in a bodily way can sometimes bring a profound *resolution* in the way the pain is carried.

This is why the behavior of felt meaning is so different from the behavior of meanings that can be conceptualized and thought. The function of felt meaning is different. It's goal is different. The most important aspect of a felt sense is not content but movement. *It is meant to unfold!*

The initial obscurity of a felt sense, your feeling something without being able to label it accurately, lies not in some as yet unnamed and murky content. It is an incompleteness that arises from the *pre-process* nature of this experience. A felt sense is much like electrical power in a wire before the switch is thrown. It is meant to go somewhere, to move, to unfold. *Felt shift,* as we mentioned earlier, is the first forward movement of an implicit meaning.

Most people who seek change in their lives look upon their feelings as either good or bad. They feel good when they are happy and challenged. They feel bad if they are depressed and anxious. Personal change is usually thought of as some sort of transformation in the *content* that is felt. But such a view is not really on target. It doesn't pinpoint the actual source of frustration.

The central issue in any blockage to human growth has relatively little to do with the content of feeling and felt meaning. But it has everything to do with whether there has been *a breakdown of movement* in the unfolding of bodily felt meaning—the *felt shift* that Gendlin has identified.

It is an over-simplification to think of personal change as some sort of magical substitution which replaces bad feelings with good ones. If looked at superficially, this may appear to be what happens whenever things get better. But close examination will show that the *restoration of inner process* is the actual vehicle of transformation.

Happiness and enhanced social awareness come about not because we have *good* feelings rather than bad ones. It is because the very basis for healthy social functioning is restored. This happens whenever bodily felt meaning which has been blocked can move forward once again. Then we become more fully functioning and more social human beings.

Felt meaning, then, is always more than the particular content which may appear to give it substance at any given moment. Like a story, *it is meant to move forward,* to lead beyond itself. A vital aspect of this meaning, then, is its potential to act as an open-ended invitation drawing each person along a path of further unfolding.

Perhaps an example can illustrate our point. The two of us enjoy going on long mountain walks in the High Sierra, and we especially appreciate pausing by the small streams that carry runoff from melting snow packs. There is something about the rush of sparkling water over smooth boulders that works a special magic on one's capacity for presence. We usually just want to sit down and be quiet for a while, not thinking about anything in particular, but simply resting in the sound and its effect upon us. Eventually, however, we reach a degree of satisfaction, and our attention is invariably drawn upstream or downstream, and we begin hiking again along the water's edge. It is this ordinary experience of walking along an unfamiliar mountain stream that might help clarify what we now recognize as an important bio-spiritual dimension to bodily knowing.

As we walk, we take time for looking. We like to stop occasionally, pick something up, view a beautiful rock formation from different angles, or enjoy the physical sensation of jumping from one dry rock to another in the midst of rushing water. Our attention is momentarily directed toward many different sights, sounds, and sensations during our hike. All this describes the immediate *content* of our experience.

But there is another, possibly an even more important dimension to this awarenss. It is the overriding *attraction* of the watercourse itself, which calls us to continue our journey up- or downstream. This attraction and the effect it has on us is like an ever-present melody or theme continually playing behind the individual stops we make to look, listen, and to admire. The stream beckons us onward because there is always a new unfolding around the next bend.

This has led us to realize that a large part of the attraction we find hiking along the water's edge is not only the individual sights we see *but the actual unfolding itself.* How often we've glanced at our watches and finding it time to turn back have felt a mingled sense of frustration, annoyance, sadness and, perhaps most of all, a kind of longing as we looked toward the next bend around which we might never travel. Reason told us that behind the disappearing curve there probably lay more of the same water, tree stumps, bushes, and wildlife. Yet somehow this logical assurance never fully satisfied us. Walking the stream has come to symbolize for us the process of life and the process we feel every person is called to experience. *Felt meaning lies not only in what is found but in the process of unfolding itself!*

The very special attraction of hiking along a stream's

edge includes not only the individual sights and sounds one stops to enjoy, but a beckoning mystery as well. It is the lure which continues to invite the traveler forward. Whenever one focuses one's attention upon particular object, *it is always done within a broader context of movement, flow, journey, process, and continuing invitation.* While our immediate attention may be directed toward an individual scene that momentarily captivates us, we never really lose our sense for the hike and for the unfolding stream that is life.

Our point, then, is that there seems to be some *body of invitation* akin to this stream experience deep within each one of us. It appears as meaning that is felt, a meaning that flows and invites us, much like our journey along the water's edge. Within this very movement a broader sense of "I" can appear.

What we are writing about in this chapter is our experience that Focusing awakens a felt sense of *process*. It unearths a knowing beyond the restrictions of *content*. Consciousness is always more than *what* we think. It is, simultaneously, a window on some wider identity. But the opening appears within the leading edge of our own personal story. Focusing helps us become aware of the movement, the *felt shift*, the *being carried forward*. It is within such an experience that we can be drawn *inside* the Mystery. This is an important realization about bio-spirituality which we have come to value over the years.

Someone once said that time, in addition to measuring motion, also has *density*. The center of a person's awareness *thickens*, so to speak, as more than separated individuality becomes involved. A person can have an awakening realization of *being within*, *being tied-into*, or *being at home within* some Larger Process.

Obviously, this is a developmental experience, a *gradual* deepening of the sense a person may have for such somatic connectedness. We always recall with fondness a personal example used by Abraham Maslow to illustrate a time when he was drawn beyond the separated world of ego. It was a story he told about himself and his family. During the wintertime the Maslows would occasionally buy strawberries as a special treat. The whole family enjoyed them. After sitting down to eat, his two little girls would gobble up their berries while Maslow and his wife dawdled over theirs. It was, as he said, a game, because he and his wife knew what would happen next. As soon as the children had finished their own berries, they looked to their parents for more. Then, Maslow said, he and his wife would feed their own strawberries one by one to their daughters and, as he put it so well: "It may sound strange, but I enjoyed the taste of the strawberries more in my child's mouth than I did in my own." The line of separation had disappeared. The dichotomy had been transcended, if you want to say it in a technical way.

What we have here is a delightful tale of expanding human experience as it travels the road toward cosmic congruence. It is an embodied sense of being carried beyond stifling individuality and separateness.

Traditional psychology naturally fits the developing person within a *chrono*logical framework—birth, infancy, childhood, adolescense, adulthood, old age, death. The Greeks called this experience of time *Chronos*. The term describes a continuum of past, present, and future. The experience of temporal succession is measured by clocks, the movement of planets, and the regular succession of day and night.

From a subjective point of view, *Chronos* refers to an experience of time in which we relate principally to the outside surfaces of things. It speaks of calculating and manipulating situations in which control is a critical ingredient. *Chronos* measures the time needed to confront and solve problems. A time in which to get things done.

But what we are trying to describe here is an aspect of the evolving sense of "I." While *Chronos* is experienced in the normal biological lifespan of each human organism, there is a still deeper movement and subjective experience that promises to transcend this more limited temporal framework.

That is perhaps why another Greek word for time found its way into New Testament usage. This term, *Kairos*, refers to a bodily-felt sense for *the time within which personal life moves forward*. *Kairos* does not describe a temporal succession but rather an inner felt motion that is associated with awakening or realization. It is an unfolding within the very center of self-awareness.

Kairos, then, does not refer to the phenomenon of being spread out laterally in time, for surviving. It refers, rather, to a process of deepening within the present moment; being drawn *inside* the movement of one's own story. It is a time not for solutions but for resolution. When it is used in the Greek New Testament, *Kairos* is linked with an experience of salvation. It is liberation from an excessively narrow and confining perception.

Focusing can never produce a *Kairos* experience on demand. That, of course, is gift. But Focusing does dispose us, position us as it reaches toward this same realm of experiencing. It seeks a cure within the person that transcends all our daily reactions.

Another kind of consciousness evolution matures within *Kairos,* right inside the growth and decline of each physical organism. This extended perception and motivation seems to aim at something beyond physical integrity and survival. Personal unfolding and change take place within a framework of *Chronos*, history, the growth and senescence of each physical organism. In a word, *the flesh*. Within this context life goes forward, the center of awareness develops, and identity undergoes continual transformation. Yet simultaneously an even more profound bio-spiritual birth can take place inside that felt movement where *Chronos,* in a sense, stands still. This is the awesome threshold of a new sense of "I."

Beyond all our daily reacting lies a self that knows the way home! Focusing can help to unveil this transforming perception. The place of *connection* lies right within the *telling* of our own stories. These two go hand in hand. We find God or the Mystery of Human Destiny within the *surprise* around each new bend of our own unfolding. As Alan Watts once wrote when commenting on religious renewal, "We do not need a new religion or a new bible. We need a new experience—a new feeling of what it is to be 'I'."[1]

George Bernard Shaw once said that by the end of the twentieth century creative evolution would become a religion. There are clues within the Christian tradition that also hint at just such an evolving fullness within the Self-Process. There is an amazing reminder of it in the New Testament that is repeated over and over again. The Christ always appears in the fullness of *Kairos!* There is a "thickening" in time and the sense of self which reaches consummation, according to the Apostle Paul, at the moment of realization in *Kairos* when God will be all in all.

While writing his Epistle to the Galatians, Saint Paul recorded his own halting steps into just such an unusual experience. In a rather remarkable utterance he exclaimed: ". . . it is no longer I who live, but Christ who lives in me. . . ." (*Gal. 2:20 RSV*) Putting aside, for now, the framework of specifically Christian belief, and considering this statement for what it appears to be—an effort to describe a deeply moving human experience—we may have a good example here of what Alan Watts was trying to describe with his call for a new sense of "I." Paul became aware that his own identity as a person was integral to the expression of a much Larger Reality. He, the separate individual, Paul, was somehow "in Christ."

The Christ, for Paul, stood as a symbol for an even greater Body of Awareness within which individual consciousness gradually unfolds. Paul's inner experience may have signalled a dawning realization for him that each apparently autonomous person, each discrete, individual particle of organic flesh also participates as an integral part of the unfolding story of a much Larger Whole. In a manner he did not fully comprehend, the Apostle found himself somehow drawn forward as a living cell within the process of this far greater organism. He experienced an advancing fullness within his own being, a development in Self-Awareness beyond anything which he as individual was capable of.

The transformation in awareness apparently came for Paul when he realized that consciousness was not limited to people's experience of their own separated fleshly selves. In a way he could only dimly comprehend, the canvas upon which he now found his identity projected was far larger than he could ever have imagined. As Paul's consciousness was drawn beyond the limited world of rational content and control into the art of allowing, his awareness gradually unfolded to include and to express some greater Self-Process.

Paul quite literally began to have a new experience of "I," discovering the focal point of his awareness and identity in something far more profound than his ordinary sense of self. Paul, from the town of Tarsus, was literally carried light years beyond the center of experiencing with which he was most familiar.

Within the framework of Christian thought the sense of self emerging within each individual appears as the tiniest visible tip of human self-realization. The process is the message, and the message is the process. Unless we consciously enter into the process that we are, we don't get the message. There remains a depth, entered precisely through the movement of unique, personal unfolding, that reveals that the limited identity that each of us experiences in daily life is grounded in a still Larger Process, the ultimate source of consciousness aware of itself.

There is a rare term of obscure meaning in the New Testament, *Pleroma*. The word signifies ripening *fullness*. A maturing within moments of *Kairos*. There is a developmental note here. For Christians, the process that God has become within human history *is not yet fully achieved*.

Look, then, to the advancing edge of your own unique story for a window on bio-spiritual awareness. Here is

where Focusing can help. It nourishes an inner bodily felt
sense of movement—resolution! Letting go and allowing,
which we wrote about earlier, encourage this seed of evolution within each one of us. They become part of the
overall climate that can carry us forward into the next
phase of consciousness. But it is the actual unfolding itself, an inner sense of one's own personhood *as process*
that is the vehicle of bio-spiritual transformation. The
mainstream of evolution operates along a broad front, and
that front passes through every human being on the face
of this globe.

"Behold, now is the acceptable time (*Kairos*)." (*2 Cor.
6:2 RSV*) When the Rosetta Stone of embodied knowing
is brought to bear upon the hidden message of Christian
revelation, attention is directed not toward some stale
content of knowledge but at the very process of felt becoming, the on-going story that each of us is at the present
moment. Within the heart of this movement lies a Greater
Word waiting to become Flesh and to dwell among us.

Chapter 6

An ancient perspective

The evolving body of spirit

Did you know that a honey bee colony functions as an *individual living organism?* All those thousands of darting forms are, in fact, a unified, integrated expression of one single, vibrating life! It's difficult to grasp this because our perception is attuned to *particularity.* We sense organisms, not The Organism. Our ability to perceive broader unities is, as yet, still undeveloped. But these are tantalizing clues. Dr. Eugene Gendlin writes:

> Your physically-felt body is in fact part of a gigantic system of here and other places, now and other times, you and other people—in fact, the whole universe. This sense of being bodily alive in a vast system is the body as it is felt from inside.[1]

What Gendlin touches on here is nothing new. Mystics have been saying the same sort of thing for centuries. But is there a bio-spiritual clue in this statement? A direction to follow? A path to explore?

Can one find here some hidden thread in the fabric of human unfolding? A slightly unravelled edge in the whole cloth? An opening through which to glimpse something of our own next step as a species on the planet earth?

It's time, now, for us to consider a few hieroglyphs in the Judaeo-Christian tradition. We can expand Gendlin's statement by entering the Semitic worldview. The purpose of this chapter is to share some information about an unusual perspective. We'll begin by looking through other people's eyes, trying to understand how they viewed the world and themselves.

There are certain refinements within the Greek New Testament, precisions which shed light upon the perennial quest for an experience of deeper unity. We shall find these precisions useful as we broaden our appreciation of what Focusing is all about.

It is interesting, at the outset, to notice the remarkable fluidity and ease with which Old and New Testament authors slip back and forth between their descriptions of an entire tribe and the individual members of it. They seem to consider each individual and the overall group as somehow one. Scripture scholars familiar with this casual juxtaposition of the individual and the larger whole speak of *corporate personality.*

Soma, a Greek term used to describe what we generally mean by *body,* has overtones of this larger incorporation. The *soma* of each person and the tribal *soma* are not only inseparable but somehow coextensive. Corporate personality exhibits much the same organicity that we have noted in the bee colony. From a Semitic perspective, the individual member of a tribe actually stands for and sums up the particular group from which he or she has sprung. *All of the whole is in the part.* You never speak of one without including the other. There is here no sense of collectivity or aggregation, no parts outside of parts, just an appreciation of some primordial organicity or *bodily felt tied-togetherness.*

Focusing, we feel, opens a doorway to this remarkable perspective. It turns a person's awareness to a point of resonance within the body where a "felt sense" for such unity resides. This is not a thinking kind of thing. It is knowing in a different way. Focusing allows our consciousness to settle into that area in ourselves where there is physical *in-binding* with the rest of the cosmos. We may, at the time, be working on some personal problem. But we are dealing with it in a *somatic* rather than in a purely logical or rational way. We are "bodying" *in* it rather than thinking *about* it. Our attention may be directed toward the felt carrying of a particular issue, but in the process we have become immersed in *soma*. We are situated in the realm of bodily felt tied-in-ness without necessarily adverting to it.

There is another interesting feature of *soma*. New Testament literature reveals a further piece of evolutionary information about this unusual perspective. Let's return once more to the honey bee colony as a way of approaching this additional revelation.

It is sad, but nonetheless true that bees no longer evolve along the *mainstream* of consciousness evolution. They are not called beyond their participation in the highly specialized colony body or *soma* which has enabled them to survive. There is no horizon to be crossed in their awareness. No beckoning adventure in consciousness. No bio-spiritual frontier. Instead, the colony is self-contained. Barring some catastrophic intervention, it is able to survive but it is no longer able to evolve.

This *self-contained* quality of *soma* is described in New Testament literature by another Greek word, *sarx*—which is literally translated as *flesh*.

Notice that *flesh* does not mean exactly the same thing as *body*. *Sarx* and *soma* are definitely related, but their New Testament use highlights a remarkable difference that goes to the heart of what bio-spirituality and Focusing are all about.

To appreciate the meaning of *sarx,* we must first note something of a primordial option faced by every subhuman species which has ever been touched by the forward thrust of evolution. In every case, the process of natural selection forced a kind of choice upon them. The option either to remain open, finding security by expanding their consciousness potential, or to close off with an efficient *specialization,* an effective *control* system which could maximize individual and species survival but only at the cost of sacrificing more open-ended awareness.

Teilhard de Chardin chronicled these events in his work as a paleontologist. The now extinct saber-toothed tiger's efficient adaptation for survival during its reign on earth also meant that it would never become the ancestor of mature human awareness. The very specialization itself, those magnificent canines and tearing claws, guaranteed a falling off from the mainstream of developing consciousness. This marvelous animal quite literally became its specialization. Awareness was frozen and conditioned by the very tools for survival, the specialization which developed through time in the *body* of this species.

Perhaps that's why it became extinct. The saber-toothed tiger could no longer adapt to a changing environment. There was not enough time in which to grow and develop a new set of tools. So the species eventually died out.

An ancient law of survival dictates that one does not casually barter hard-won gains on the playing field of life. There is strength and endurance in this. Continuity and direction emerge when the basics of survival are assured.

But there are perils as well. *Success often limits flexibility!* Attitudes and approaches harden. In a world where *development* is the norm, effective specialization frequently narrows the possibility for consciousness evolution. Survival, it seems, can be purchased at the expense of expanding awareness.

The primary axis of evolution must then turn elsewhere for a point of further breakthrough, seeking yet another interface where an openness for further advance can be found. Like water flowing downhill, evolution searches out the path of least resistance, *flowing wherever consciousness is, less conditioned by the specializations with which it survives!*

It is clear that the option to accept or reject this forward advance of consciousness is now, for us humans, *a choice*. Our organismic specializations for survival are no longer exclusively physical but psychological. Human beings are efficient toolmakers. We do not grow antlers or cloven hooves, specialized canines or claws. Our tools are not physically *built-in* to our bodies. The hand with its opposable thumb means that we can make a diversity of instruments which are separate from ourselves. We are freed from this kind of elementary choice or natural selection.

A human being's primordial options now lie more within the heart. The blessing here is that they are *more flexible*. These choices are not irrevocable. Once the antler has grown, once the claws are in place, *there is no turning back* for that species. For us, however, there is space for maneuvering. Our psychological specializations are more malleable. But the eventual choice still has overtones of our evolutionary origins. We are doing basically the same thing. We must opt for continued openness and advance or isolating closure, control, and specialization.

Carried to an extreme, voluntary closure in the human being marks the appearance of what biblical tradition speaks of as *sin*. When sin is looked at from a broader evolutionary view rather than from a narrow moral point of view, it means slipping away from the mainstream of advancing consciousness and deserting the bio-spiritual quest. It is a tragic option within the forward flow of ourselves, and there is profound social as well as personal heartbreak in such calamitous decisions. By refusing to be our own unfolding stories, we thereby diminish not only our isolated selves but also the unified thrusting of consciousness within all of humankind.

That is why the Bible poses another dramatic option to sustain the forward thrust of human evolution. It speaks of *metanoia,* conversion. A return to the way. It is a coming home once again in openness to the unfolding inner destiny which calls us ahead. It is a radical choice for the risks of development rather than secure specialization and control as the more profound response to being human.

Focusing occurs along this cutting edge of conversion and evolution within every person. There is a letting go and dropping of the reins. *Allowing* some power beyond all our secure specializations to lead us ahead. Focusing takes place in the flesh (*sarx*) because it deals with a "felt" sense. But at the same time it looks beyond the flesh. Beyond self-containment. It reveals another potential, another capability that transcends all our striving for control. Beyond individual survival lies a further possibility: the transforming call to *evolve!*

Sarx, then, is the body of fleshly specialization. It is *soma* (whether individual, or extended like the bee colony) that is geared for survival, but it is not necessarily open to the further call of consciousness evolution. *Sarx* is self-containment, the *healthy* drive toward self-determination, maintenance of biological integrity, and psychological automony.

We stress the word *healthy* because specialization and control are, obviously, necessary for biological survival. But human life is more than simply surviving. There is development and evolution as well. *Sarx* is only one element in an overall pattern of advancing consciousness. It is a vital ingredient, but it is only a part of the picture.

This experience of consciousness is necessarily mortal. Individuals die. Species fade away. The *soma* of *sarx* is a fleshly body of death and decay. It is the vehicle of consciousness *for a time*. It is fragile and limited.

But the New Testament describes something more. It reveals dramatic new perspective on the process of human evolution. It tells of an awareness of greater connectedness and organicity that appears within the *unfinished* character of human existence. It is to this unfinished edge that Focusing directs our attention.

St. Paul and St. John describe the gradual unfolding of *a new soma!* An advancing Body of awareness that appears within the maturing of consciousness itself. Here, at last, one awakens to the realm of bio-spirituality.

Not only is there species-wide kinship in the flesh (*sarx*), a common rootedness in some greater *soma* of human mortality. There is also an incredible bond *in our very openness to evolution!* The human species is *somatic* in its self-containment *as well as* in its potential for further advance.

The New Testament seeks to describe a further dimension to *soma* that is of unimaginable magnitude and depth. It points to a radically transformed basis for human identity which carries us light years beyond our most cherished ties with the earth.

Just as *somatic* organicity bonds us to our fleshly origins in the drama of earth's rise to reflex awareness, so too, there appears to be an organicity in the forward flow of consciousness itself. The dawn of *a new soma* with roots and drawing power in something beyond self-contained survival.

The New Testament has a word to describe this emerging *soma* as it appears on the leading edge of the many stories which we are. It is *Pneuma*—Spirit. A *soma* of expanding human awareness. This remarkable word has been used throughout Christian literature to describe *the on-goingness, the open-endedness* of each person's individual story. It is the species-wide movement toward greater tied-in-ness. A *gift* which draws consciousness forward.

My life, *my* reason for existing, *my* unique story is always more than the repetition of a dead-ended specialization. My story is no tired tale of past survival and success. It is my ongoing journey into the greater fleshly body of *sarx* as well as into the exciting edge of gift that leads me still further ahead. There is a mysticism of nature that bonds all things in the common heritage of earth and stars—and yet, there is something more.

A Spirit of the Earth! An eruption within *sarx*. The

bursting forth of a seed resisting all entropy and decay. We are all *sarx*—together with the earth from which we spring. But we are *pneuma* as well. We are drawn forward by that gifted power working through aeons of evolution that has brought us to this point in ourselves—and now leads still further beyond.

Christian tradition refers to this process as *a resurrection of the flesh*. The transcending of limited, self-contained survival. It is being drawn beyond the narrow world of control.

Focusing addresses this miracle as an integral part of daily living. Resurrection is *now!* It is developmentally present as the grain of mustard seed. The Kingdom of Heaven is within. Focusing can help find the vague, dim outline of this incredible Body of Spirit. A power beyond all *sarx*.

There have been serious misunderstandings throughout Christian history about the true meaning of *flesh*. It has been loudly condemned by some. A forlorn figure at the mercy of prim rectitude and narcissistic self-righteousness. Yet despite these frenetic outbursts of self-rejection where the over-riding preoccupation of Christian experience has all too often glorified a denial of *sarx,* the drama of Incarnation has never been completely obscured. Like a tender crocus in the springtime, it has endured the harsh winter of incredulity and religious abuse. The prologue to St. John's gospel can never be denied: "And the Word became Flesh (*sarx*) and dwelt among us." (*John, 1:14 RSV*) For the Christian, whatever there is of Mystery and transcendence in human life, it must necessarily be bound up with *sarx*. This basically open organism of ours, this heaving, sighing, singing mass of emotion and wonderment, courage and cowardice, passion, self-sacrifice and indifference is a crucible for the next forward step into who we ultimately are.

There is a profound vision of human possibility in the writings of St. Paul and St. John, a salvation history of cosmic proportion which sums up what we have briefly described of corporate personality, *soma, sarx,* and *pneuma.* All these elements come together into a challenging picture of *the possible human.*

The unified *soma* of humanity in *sarx* is the biblical *Adam!* For Christian believers, all of humankind is the body of Adam, the corporate personality of our fleshly origin. But because we can evolve, because the primary axis of consciousness evolution still courses through our human unfolding, we are opened in this gifted advance to perceive and to participate in the birth of a New Adam, a new corporate personality and *Soma* called *Christ.*

Teilhard de Chardin used the term *Christo-genesis* to describe the *developmental* character of this Larger Body. He highlighted *the awakening* of a new *Soma.* "Body of Christ" names a transformation within the depth of human awareness itself.

A new Copernican revolution is now breaking upon the frontiers of consciousness. As humankind has been forced to relocate its place among the stars, it must now by the overwhelming demand of consciousness readjust its very perception of God. Dramatic in its consequences, we are entering a profound reorientation in perspective. It is a vital challenge for the Christian community. From the vantage point of human development, *the experience of Christian revelation is not first about God—but about ourselves!* Within an evolutionary framework, Trinity, Incarnation, Grace, Faith, Sacrament, and Christology—all are meant to describe an unfolding of human consciousness. They highlight aspects of *human self-awareness and human self-process.*

In this sense, then, a rediscovered Christian biospirituality could contain a message of incalculable value for the advancement of human evolution. There is information here. A vast, hidden message. But to experience this incredible resource, the Rosetta Stone of bodily awareness must be brought to bear upon precious clues in this ancient tradition. This leap into the body's knowing, however, has been tragically lost within most of Christianity today.

Yet perhaps the vision of Teilhard de Chardin and what might be described as the pragmatic mysticism of Eugene Gendlin can excite further exploration of this neglected realm within ourselves. Pere Teilhard was well aware of the dynamic surge within consciousness as it responded to a call beyond the limited *soma* of nature's self-contained survival. Gendlin has reaffirmed that steps in the direction of this Larger Mystery are steps always taken within the richness of *sarx*. The Flesh! Our inner window on *pneuma* (spirit) is set in the world of *sensory awareness*, that marvelous tapestry of *meaning that can be felt*. It is here that the gift which draws us ahead is known as an incarnation, an enfleshment. An eventual resurrection.

Focusing looks toward just such *somatic* knowing. More than simply getting in touch with one's feelings, it seeks a unique edge in awareness where fresh new possibilities can emerge. Focusing identifies an opening within the fabric of human unfolding. It marks a way through to the Body of Spirit!

Chapter 7

The body's approach to death

A story being born in every dying

Imagine what it would be like to be a tiny, unobtrusive observer within the womb when a new life was being formed. Over a period of nine months you could see the gradual growth of cells, muscle, bone, and tissue. The formation of tiny arms, legs, hands, and the emergence of facial features would be a marvel to behold. As growth progressed and life's miracle developed, a time would come when the spontaneous movement of a hand or foot would occur and you could thrill to what was taking place before you.

Then, at the appointed hour, there would be a terrific straining of muscles, the breaking of membranes, a gushing of fluids, and suddenly *life would be gone!* The womb would be empty, leaving only tattered remnants of a throbbing aliveness which you had been privileged to observe during the long period of gestation. From your restricted point of view, you would have to conclude that the life had gone out. It was no more. *It had died.*

Being confined within the womb would severely limit your perspective. Unless you began to sense that the bodily formation taking place before you was somehow organized for life *outside* the womb, the cataclysmic departure could only be viewed as an end to everything. The quintessence of death itself.

However, a very perceptive observer might get some inkling of the larger life-process which the fetus was destined for by examining the limbs and sense organs as they matured in preparation for life *outside* the womb. These feet were made for walking! These eyes were made for seeing! This nose was made for breathing—but not in the warm, dark, watery womb.

Tiny feet, hands, nose, eyes, and ears all tell the perceptive observer something about what is yet to come. They represent *traces* within a limited uterine perspective of what lies beyond the next horizon. They are harbingers of the sensory world ahead.

This womb image came to us during a period of concentrated Focusing in preparation for the funeral of a dear friend. While we were sitting quietly with all the memories and felt knowing that stirred within us, we waited until this thought-provoking symbol brought about a shift in our bodily awareness. A felt transition in how the event could be carried.

The fear of death can be resolved in our bodies, not solved with our minds. There is no *answer* to the dreadful specter of total annihilation. No *solution* which soothes the mind's shattered logic. But there is response within the body. A felt naturalness, perhaps even rightness, about the experience, as though some inward organismic knowing recognizes death as a vital transition. Something is born in every dying! A believing is born of change.

Focusing can begin to transform one's perception, not through an *explanation* of death, but by providing a different place to stand within ourselves. This shift in perspective may itself be the answer which so many people seek.

Focusing draws our awareness toward the inner world of bodily meaning and felt movement. We approach death through a different kind of knowing. There is no bright flame of rationality here with which to pierce the gloom of dying. Just a *felt conviction* that grows to become far more satisfying than all the feverish explanations which reason can provide.

When Teilhard de Chardin reflected on the probable coming of an "ultra-humanity," he challenged us to look beyond the narrow perceptual framework with which we are so familiar. His conclusion as a paleontologist was that

> ... our present condition is still so immature that Mankind in its existing form ... cannot be scientifically regarded as anything more than an organism which has not yet emerged from the embryonic stage.[1]

Perhaps even now we feel this womb-like condition. All around us the periphery of consciousness fades off into dark unknowing. Reason can never penetrate this inky void. But our bodies, in their own way, may see farther than we realize.

There is an initial awareness in the feet, hands, and eyes of every fetus before birth. Some dim perception of purpose and finality. Perhaps a yearning to exercise the functions for which they have been fashioned.

Can our bodies even now hint at such subtle knowing? Is there a "language" deep within present experience that yields a *trace* of wider awareness? Are we on the road toward yet another birth? The light of a new day dawning?

Occasionally, in our reading of certain creative authors we have been touched by passages that speak of a wider scope of human consciousness. Suddenly a passage leaps out with a bodily-felt drawing power and energy far beyond the matter-of-fact information it may contain. For example, William James, in a cautious statement that concludes his monumental work on *The Varieties of Re-*

ligious Experience, summarized his findings about such an experience as follows:

> Disregarding the over-beliefs, and confining ourselves to what is common and generic, we have in *the fact that the conscious person is continuous with a wider self through which saving experiences come,* a positive content of religious experience which, it seems to me, *is literally and objectively true as far as it goes.*[2]

While reading this passage for the first time, we were struck by James' notion of continuity with some "wider self." Our response was immediate and tangibly organic. Something felt right about the statement as, in much the same fashion, it might feel right for a fetus to flex its muscles and kick in the womb without really knowing what such kicking was about.

This is not a rightness which is easily analyzed with logic and reason. It cannot be reduced to categories of cause and effect. Yet something in the body feels at home with such a statement. At least it did for us.

On another occasion several years ago we had been reading Dom Sebastian Moore's challenging book, *God Is a New Language.* A passage stood out at that time and is still vivid to us:

> The human body is not a sort of super-expensive toy. It is very misleading to call it *your* body: to exist in the body means to be bound by a thousand ties into the whole bundle of existence. This inbinding, which is beyond our personal control, is *us* just as much as what we call "I" is us.[3]

Again, the same felt wonder, and the feeling of being on target. The body said "Yes!" in a way quite unlike what the mind might say. The felt meaning of this passage, for us, was far different from any *thinking* of it. There was deeper resonance. Some untapped reserve of knowing was called into play.

On another occasion we were reading from Karl Rahner's article "Christology and an Evolutionary World View." Again, the same felt sense emerged.

> Matter is presently at a stage where, in man, it is conscious of itself and of its relation to reality as a whole and to the source of its existence. . . . The material world is to some extent the one body of a manifold self-consciousness incorporating that body into the relation to its infinite source. And if cosmic consciousness has reached its first step in man, it must continue to develop. Through his body man is allied to the whole cosmos and communicates with it. In their role as reference point of the spirit, body and cosmos together press on to ever greater consciousness.[4]

Our response to this somewhat academic philosophical reflection was later felt with even greater intensity when we were reading a brief passage from the theoretical physicist, Sir Arthur Eddington. His novel view of ultimate reality once again sparked in us a deeper felt meaning. The written conclusion found a receptive audience within the body's sense for direction and purpose in the cosmos.

> To put the conclusion crudely, the stuff of the world is mind stuff. . . . consciousness is not sharply defined, but fades into sub-consciousness and beyond that we must postulate something indefinite but yet continuous with our mental nature. . . . it is difficult for the matter of fact physicist to accept the view that the substratum of everything is of mental character. . . .
>
> Not in the dim past but continuously by conscious mind is the miracle of creation wrought. The idea of a universal Mind or Logos would be, I think, a fairly

plausible inference from the present state of scientific theory; at least it is in harmony with it. . . . religion first became possible for a reasonable scientific man about the year 1927.[5]

We recall a film about severely disturbed children who were being cared for in a family-style setting, seven or eight youngsters living in a house with two adult counselors. In one memorable scene a nine-year-old boy climbed to the top of a tall cabinet and refused to come down. He was yelling obscenities at everyone within earshot like a little rooster crowing from the rooftop. The counselors cajoled, bantered with him, and even taunted him. Gradually, the edge of humor began to creep in. The small, fiercely determined youngster would yell, scream, and then turn away to giggle. An obscenity would end on a half-repressed laugh. The counselors knew what was happening and kept the process going. Finally the boy allowed himself to be pulled down to a loving hug with one more layer removed from his protective armor. A small step was taken away from the darkness of egoism. A brief flash of salvation, like a welcome meteor brightened the dark night of a tiny, tortured life. Faith, at last, had arrived. The believing born of change. With humor and love came a friendlier place inside. The inner landscape was different.

Each of the passages we have just cited called forth a similar friendly space—a point of cosmic connectedness within bodily knowing. The specter of death is resolved in the body, not solved with the mind. That is the leap of faith. We wonder, now, whether such gifted moments represent a trace of broader awareness, some felt sense for "a wider self through which saving experiences come."

There is an interesting clue in the Bible about such an expanding experience. The hint comes from another special word in the Greek New Testament. St. Paul writes of such Larger Awareness as *Musterion*, The Mystery. *Musterion* is the greater Whole within which we fit as parts. Yet, at the same time, this greater Whole is expressed *in* us. All of the Whole is in every part.

Ordinarily, *Musterion* is translated into the Latin scriptures as *Mysterium,* "Mystery." But occasionally another word is used instead: *Sacramentum.* Our English word *sacrament* comes from this. It is sometimes translated in the New Testament as "secret" or "hidden purpose."

> He has made known to us his hidden purpose [*Musterion/Sacramentum*]—such was his will and pleasure determined beforehand in Christ—to be put into effect when the time [*Kairos*] was ripe [*Pleroma*]: namely, that the universe, all in heaven and on earth, might be brought into a unity in Christ. (*Eph. 1:9-10 NEB*)

Most Christians think of Sacrament as one of the seven sacraments like Baptism or Matrimony. But there is a broader psychological sense behind the meaning of this sign/action. Sacraments exist within the Christian community in order to foster an awareness of the innate sacramentality of human existence itself.

There is hidden purpose within the gift of life. There is a secret *interface* through which one can be drawn forward toward greater awareness. A sacramental attitude is essentially one of openness to this larger picture, an inner appreciation of the movement which draws us ahead. It involves a commitment to living in that movement. One may refer to this unfolding as Body of Spirit or the Self-Process, but what sacrament really implies is an alertness for signs of hidden purpose. There is an expectation that every act, every thought, no matter how ordinary, offers a potential doorway to our own and the world's evolution.

This reminds us of an image that Pete often uses. One day while he was seated at his desk, he was idly looking out the window after a rainstorm. Droplets of water dotted the pane in front of him. As the sun came out from behind a cloud, Pete watched the play of light and color in the drops. Suddenly he realized that each drop of water contained the same image reflected from outside the window. The corner of our house was clearly visible in every drop. Each contained an image of this larger whole. Each reflected that whole. Each was an avenue of access to something beyond itself. The sacramental side of human existence speaks of this underlying connection.

If there is promise of immortality and some potential for identity continuity which even now transcends the grim prospect of final extinction, it will most probably be found in whatever we can experience of sacramental unfolding within ourselves. Here at last we may find a potential "lookout point in the universe," some hint in our womb-like existence of greater life to come.

There is profound sacramentality at work in Focusing whenever the felt sense unfolds. A connection appears within that very movement which carries us forward. The "felt shift." Because there is a letting go, a kind of dying, new life can appear. Death followed by resurrection.

But this Larger Picture unfolds within the living flesh (*sarx*) of each individual person, much as the image of our house appeared whole and intact within each raindrop. Individuality, therefore, is the stuff within which this greater awareness occurs. Uniqueness is important. It can never be abandoned.

Focusing, perhaps, can unveil this sacramental opening within our inner universe. There is a subtle trace of light which indicates that the darkness of our womb-like and all-too-often separated existence is only a prelude to an even greater awakening.

Death for us humans may be a kind of ultimate sacrament, a final step into the body's knowing which reveals some "hidden purpose," a friendly place on the far side of ego. There is a seed within *sarx*, *a secret* waiting to burst forth within the very consciousness that rebels against dying.

Is each of us an unfolding "felt sense" within some Greater Awareness? Does a Deeper Source, a Wider Self, a Universal Mind or Logos *focus upon us* as the personal edge of its own unique unfolding? Are we raindrops on some cosmic window, extending consciousness one step further into the darkness of matter itself?

Should death be feared any more than some timorous felt sense might shrink from the rush of awareness carrying it forward toward greater Fullness (*Pleroma*) in personal unfolding? What, after all, does our bodily felt meaning really have to fear? *It is already one with that which it is in the process of becoming!*

Chapter 8

Toward a new paradigm for Western spirituality

Carl Jung once described a tragic irony he had observed in the lives of many Christians.

> That I feed the hungry, that I forgive an insult, that I love my enemy in the name of Christ—all these are undoubtedly great virtues. What I do unto the least of my brethren, that I do unto Christ. But what if I should discover that the least amongst them all, the poorest of all the beggars, the most impudent of all the offenders, the very enemy himself—that these are within me, and that I myself stand in need of the alms of my own kindness—that I myself am the enemy who must be loved—what then? As a rule, the Christian's attitude is then reversed; there is no longer any question of love or long-suffering; we say to the brother within us "Raca," and condemn and rage against ourselves. We hide it from the world; we refuse to admit ever having met this least among the lowly in ourselves. Had it been God himself who drew near to us in this despicable form, we should have denied him a thousand times before a single cock had crowed.[1]

What a paradox! What an enigma that this disabling experience should be fed by the paralyzing impotence of Christian spirituality whenever it confronts the specter of self-hatred. Instead of responding with a healing *process,* what is provided, instead, is information. This sort of approach is misguided and ineffective. The articulation of ideals and values, the teaching of biblical narratives, explaining theological truths about God's love and the "saying of prayers" do not create the psychological climate and quality of self-presence within which human wholeness and a more loving person can emerge. Responding with religious ideas and ideals does not support that leap into body consciousness that spirituality, love, and human maturing are really all about. As a result, the love which so many sincere Christians want to share with others they can hardly extend to themselves.

Christian spirituality has yet to resolve this split between loving one's neighbor and loving one's self. Churches still do not understand that all the preaching and teaching of theological truths and ideals will not make this problem go away. The neglect of body consciousness is an enormous obstacle both to human maturing as well as to spiritual growth. Jung always hoped that some day Christianity would recognize the body's integral role in consciousness evolution and spiritual development.

> . . . if we can reconcile ourselves with the mysterious truth that spirit is the living body seen from within, and the body the outer manifestation of the living spirit—the two being really one—then we can understand why it is that the attempt to transcend the present level of consciousness must give its due to the body.[2]

Christian spirituality, however, still lacks an effective praxis that can bring these two together within experience. Whatever direction pastoral ministry and spirituality may travel in the future, they will certainly need to address the continuing tragedy of self-hatred in a far more effective fashion. Radical change will be necessary if a new paradigm for Western spirituality is to emerge from Christianity. Without drastic course correction, this ancient tradition will simply go on contributing to the problem rather than offering an effective solution.

Any theology that is compatible with the human growth process is still only information. As such, it remains powerless to effect transformation when pain, fear, and self-hatred are present and carried in our bodies. Every such attitude, after all, grows out of *a felt sense*. The fear and rejection which so many people feel toward themselves can only be healed by owning and listening to the bodily-felt sense out of which all this negativity arises.

Christian churches, of course, are not the only places where this bodily felt awareness is tragically ignored. A far broader cultural neglect extends this attitude into health care, education, politics, social programs, and penal institutions. But the churches may be in a unique position to bring about significant social change if they can first put their own houses in order. Any new paradigm for Western spirituality must actually take a leap into body consciousness rather than simply talking about it theologically.

This need to heal self-hatred highlights one of the critical issues facing Western spirituality. Our human survival depends upon the resolution of this catalyst for massive self-destruction. But there is yet another problem of enormous significance for growth and survival.

We turn once again to Carl Jung for a concise statement of the issue. It surfaced in a comment he made on the relationship between yoga and Christianity.

Jung clearly identifies a lopsided mind-set which any effective Western spirituality must counteract. We call attention to this limited perspective because it can also distort and frustrate the Focusing process.

Western man has no need of more superiority over nature, whether outside or inside. He has both in almost devilish perfection. What he lacks is conscious recognition of his inferiority to the nature around and within him. He must learn that he may not do exactly as he wills. . . . Since Western man can turn everything into a technique, it is true in principle that everything that looks like a method is either dangerous or condemned to futility. Insofar as yoga is a form of hygiene, it is as useful to him as any other system. In the deepest sense, however, yoga does not mean this but, if I understand it correctly, a great deal more, namely the final release and detachment of consciousness from all bondage to object and subject. . . . My criticism is directed solely against the application of yoga to the peoples of the West. . . . Western civilization is scarcely a thousand years old and must first of all free itself from its barbarous one-sidedness. This means, above all, deeper insight into the nature of man. But no insight is gained by repressing and controlling the unconscious, and least of all by imitating methods which have grown up under totally different psychological conditions. In the course of the centuries the West will produce its own yoga, and it will be on the basis laid down by Christianity.[3]

Yoga, for Jung, is more than mere mental hygiene. It is, in his view, the disciplined commitment to that gift of consciousness and experience which lies beyond the realm of deliberate control. For this reason he regarded the Western tendency to acquire control through technique as a serious obstacle to human/spiritual maturity.

We raise this issue because the overwhelming need for power over nature can introduce a subtle temptation even into the Focusing process. It is a temptation which grows stronger with each successful application to the crises and brush fires of daily life. A person can gradually come to regard his or her Focusing as nothing more than *technique*. A convenient tool. Something done in order to feel better. Before long, Focusing can be directed toward inner hurts much as one applies medicine to a wound. Little by little it becomes natural to try to turn this activity into *a new form of control*. No step-by-step psychological process is immune from this kind of misuse, even one whose essential psychological dynamic is the letting go of control. Focusing, too, can become just one more instance of a "Western" approach to "the nature within and around us."

The catch, however, is that for Focusing to work, a person must first *let go* of the need to be in charge of each felt sense. And as soon as a person finally does let go and experiences resolution in bodily knowing, something deep inside usually wants control over this very process so that it can be repeated again and again at will. This is a strange paradox, this creeping back into awareness of a desire for greater control by "letting go."

But the success of Focusing lies in treating it as far more than a technique that we do on our own. *Focusing becomes an effective agent of healing transformation not because we do it, but insofar as we, finally, can allow it to do itself!*

This is not mere playing with words. Something radically different operates throughout the Focusing process. "Letting go" and "allowing" unveil a new horizon within bodily knowing. People who live with this dimension of themselves every day gradually come to relish being surprised by what their bodies know about meaning and direction in life. In time, a dedication and commitment can develop toward making space for this transformed way of being.

As this happens, we find Focusing valued in a different way. While still prized as a helpful approach for dealing with difficult things, it is cherished even more as a doorway of bio-spiritual awareness. Out of this experience deeper questions of meaning can be addressed.

Focusing offers a practical alternative to those spiritual practices which fail to resolve the destruction and pain of self-hatred. It opens a doorway into the body that is rich in an experience of mystery, gift, and surprise. But the one who focuses must grow in the realization that bodily knowing is filled with more than what we achieve by the power of our own hands. Focusing directly counteracts the mind-set of which Jung wrote earlier, but not without the continuing disposition of "letting go."

Before bringing this book to a close, let us briefly share a final reflection on why we believe Focusing, together with certain ancient teachings in the Judaeo-Christian tradition, can make a significant contribution to an evolving new paradigm for Western spirituality.

The "rediscovery" of the body in our age and culture has opened a critical threshold in spiritual awareness. A dialogue, hopefully, will soon begin between an ancient faith struggling to find its voice in this age of perpetual transition and the ring of a fresh new humanism that reaches for faithfulness to its own deepest yearnings. In union with one another they must find some way to go beyond the overriding need for control as well as that hardening core of fear, mistrust, and self-hatred which permeates so many lives today and threatens the specter of a nuclear nightmare.

One theologian, Gregory Baum, has tried to express the presence of God in a new language. It is a language that is as understandable to the modern humanist as it can be to a believer in an ancient tradition. He writes of prayer, a somewhat undervalued commodity in our modern, secular world. Undervalued, that is, until each of us senses within our own life struggle the neglected message of Western spirituality.

To pray is to be in touch with oneself in a new way: to listen to the melody, not made by ourselves, that sounds at the core of our being and, from beyond the sickness that deafens us, summons us to be alive.

Since God is redemptively present in man's coming
to be, prayer is a way of holding or possessing oneself.
This kind of prayer is not a moving away from oneself
and reaching out for another, but rather a being in
communion with oneself across many obstacles, and
a laying hold of oneself in and through the gift dimension that is constitutive of one's being.[4]

Baum describes the sheer organicity of grace at work in
bodily knowing. The kingdom of heaven is within. It is a
"gift dimension that is constitutive of one's being."

Abraham Maslow echoed much the same sentiment.

A whole school of psychologists now believe that
"spiritual values" are *in* the organism, so much a part
of the well-functioning organism as to be *sine qua
non* "defining-characteristics" of it.[5]

What links Western science with the Judaeo-Christian tradition is the common ground of bodily knowing.
Here there is room for a mutual bio-spiritual perspective.
A common "lookout point in the universe." Focusing helps
awaken an organismic sense for some inner power and
gift beyond anything that we could ever contrive. It is
coming in touch "across many obstacles" with a melody
that calls us to life. Focusing opens the possibility that a
process of resolution may go forward *in our bodies*. From
a Christian perspective, this is the stuff of *grace* and *incarnation*. This is not more information, but touching and
being touched by the very realities which theology describes so abstractly.

Christianity has preserved a wisdom tradition about
"the gift dimension of our being." It is not only information, but experience as well. Yet these riches have hardly
been tapped. And there is still so much more: the appreciation of *Soma* and Spirit; a tied-in-ness to cosmos and
beyond; a marvelous sense for movement, development,
and an unfolding into the inner life of God. We are all,

according to Christian revelation, the Body of Adam and—within some vast evolutionary unfolding—an emerging *Soma* of Christ. We are bound together by *chronos* and *sarx* (the flesh), yet touched by the fullness of time in *kairos*. The kingdom of heaven *is* within. But a way home to realizing all this still sleeps soundly inside bodily knowing. The Rosetta Stone of consciousness has only been barely unearthed.

If there is common ground between Maslow and Baum it lies in their mutual respect for the human body and some sense, however vague, for the "gift dimension of our being." Much within the Christian tradition still remains hidden from the perspective of bodily knowing. But the experience of *gift* and a commitment to *incarnating presence* within the felt sense of each passing moment—that is readily available. Now!

Grace and Incarnation. One can begin here the quest for a new paradigm, the search for a uniquely Western yoga. We are coming home, finally, to the Mystery of Body Consciousness/God Consciousness.

Appendix 1

A summary
of Focusing steps
as we teach them

You will find outlined below the steps of Focusing along with a few practical suggestions about what to do if someone can't get a felt sense or if the felt sense doesn't express itself. Under each step of Focusing, we suggest some statements and questions which may be used when Focusing alone or when helping another person.

If two people are doing this together, one Focusing and the other acting as facilitator, it helps to have clear ground rules. The one Focusing should always let the facilitator know when he or she has completed a step. The facilitator can then read the instructions for the next step.

Sometimes when a symbol comes to express the felt sense, it may be of such a private nature that the one Focusing would feel uncomfortable sharing it. If this should happen, it is helpful to have agreed beforehand that in this case instead of sharing the actual symbol that comes, the focuser might say something like: "I have a symbol." This alerts the facilitator that the focuser has come upon something that he or she would rather not reveal. The facilitator can then ask: "Is that symbol something you would like to be more in touch with at this time?" If the answer is Yes, the facilitator can then help the focuser to *be in* the felt sense of all about that symbol, whatever it may be.

In a case like this, the one Focusing preserves his or her privacy. At another time, a symbol may come that it feels OK to make public. And so it is shared with the facilitator.

It is possible, however, for an entire Focusing session to take place in which the facilitator has absolutely no knowledge of the *content* which the focuser is working on. The facilitator should realize that his or her role is *to support a process*. Nothing more. He or she is *not* there to provide content input for the focuser. The role of the facilitator is not to make cognitive connections of insight but to support a forward movement of felt meaning within the person who focuses.

The wordings of the instructions and questions in the following summary are only suggestions. There is no one way to lead someone through Focusing nor to do it oneself. Each person must find his or her own way of saying and presenting what is there. It is important, however, to include all the steps as they are listed—especially in the beginning. Be sure *never* to omit Step #3, "Is it OK to be with this?" until you sense that you and the person you may be helping have focused enough so that you can quite literally "be with *anything*" in yourself.

The essence of Focusing is in Steps #4 and #5: "Letting go into it" and "Allowing it to express itself." Sometimes a person will need an inventory and enough time to feel which is Number One. Sometimes they will *know* without any preliminaries what needs to be focused on. If this happens, just check to make sure it's OK to be with it before moving directly into Steps #4 and #5.

There are also some ground rules given below about concluding a Focusing session with another person which may prove helpful. When you're helping someone, it's good not to have them stop in a bad place, hanging on the edge of a cliff, so to speak. Focusing will usually run in a cycle, working through a difficulty and then gradually arriving through bodily resolution at some better place.

If you are running out of time, you might ask, upon arriving at a natural resting place, "Is this something you would like to go further with, or would it be OK to stop here for now?" Generally we find it better to propose the option about proceeding further with Focusing rather than abruptly stopping the process. What you, as facilitator, regard as a natural stopping place may not be such for the one Focusing.

If at any point you become unsure about what to do next, ask the one Focusing: "What does it feel right to do now?"

Remember, the person Focusing is *always* the one in charge! If he or she wants to stop, stop! If they run into something that is too scary to go further with and they decide to back off, that's their choice. Let them back off. You, as facilitator, might suggest at that point something like: "Would it be all right just to be with how scary this is getting now and the need to back away from it?" Help the person stay with whatever comes as a real felt meaning right now.

Remember, too, that you want to help the focuser find some way to be with negative feelings and issues that is different from their usual holding them at arm's length or trying to avoid them. Being *friendly* with an issue means that at least for this Focusing session you try being open to all that is there without immediately seeking to control it, make it better, or make it go away. Feelings change *as* they unfold, *as* they are heard, *as* they tell their own uniquely felt stories. The concrete imagery of putting something painful on one's lap and holding it as one might hold a hurting child may be helpful for some. Others, perhaps, will find that this involves too much closeness or that such an image does not appeal to them. Encourage the focuser to discover his or her own special way of "putting a friendly arm around" all the body experiencing of an issue that usually is held at arm's length.

Sometimes, when the one you are helping seems to be getting nowhere, it often helps to stop Focusing for a bit and, if it feels right, let the person talk about whatever he or she is trying to get close to. Your task will be to listen in a very special way.

Don't engage in an ordinary conversation in which you share your own opinions, comments, judgments, evaluations, and so on. Rather, try to let the other person know that you really hear each point they are making, and especially each feeling you perceive in what is being shared.

The two of us like to call this kind of caring presence *healing listening*. It is a way of being with another person in which you are present for their sake and not seeking to push some hidden agenda of your own.

When you are doing healing listening, you might find it helpful to ask yourself the following question: "How is this other person *in* what he or she is saying?" What you seek to become aware of is not merely the *content* being shared—*what* is being talked about—but, rather, *how this person must be feeling inside the experience he or she is narrating*. Scared, angry, upset, and so forth? You, as healing listener, then respond not to *what* has been said but *how* this person feels in what is being shared. Let the person know that you hear their excitement, desperation, loneliness, frustration, jealousy, or whatever.

Then when both of you catch the edge of some more prominent feeling which may arise during this sharing, you might ask: "Is that something you would like to be with for a bit and Focus on?" if the answer is Yes, check first to make sure it's OK to be with this, and then move right into Step #4.

Remember, Focusing is a very personal, caring, and gentle way of being with yourself or another person. We might even use the word *reverent*. It is not *pushing* to get somewhere. Remember also, that even though you think

you know what needs to happen in another person or yourself, the body's wisdom rarely follows a path laid down by the mind. You are doing something quite *different* when you Focus. *Allowing* a process to go forward. You're leaving yourself open to be drawn in a direction you might never have previously considered. You're sitting down next to what hurts in you or what your body tells you is Number One, and waiting for the possibility of change.

You won't hurt yourself or the other person when you try to be present in this loving, caring manner. Within the space created by such allowing, you simply wait for direction to emerge from within. What can be harmful, however, is your stumbling in with ill-timed advice or with judgments and evaluations that really don't *assist the process*.

There is a time and a place for such critical evaluation. But when you are trying to help yourself or another person become unstuck within a deeper realm of bodily meaning, the rules of the game are changed. Here, remember, the horse in you knows its way far better than you do!

FOCUSING STEPS
(as we teach them)

1. *Finding a Space by Taking an Inventory*

A) Take a few moments to grow quiet (pause) and then let your attention settle into the center of your body, noticing how you feel inside. (pause) Gradually allow this inside awareness to extend to the rest of your body, noting whatever might be there. (pause)

B) Now, let me know if something comes when you ask yourself: "Is there anything in my life right now keeping me from feeling really good?" (pause)

> *If the focuser doesn't respond after some time, the facilitator might ask: "Did anything surface?" If the answer is Yes go to (C); if the answer is No go to (E).*

C) All right, now, see if you can set this whole thing on the floor beside you for the time being; and let me know if you are able to do this.

> *If the person can't set it down, you might ask if he or she can be gentle and try again, letting you know if it is possible to set it down. If it cannot be set down, go to Step #3 and ask if it would be OK to sit quietly and focus on this.*

> *If the person can set it down, then say:*

Take a moment to get the feel of what it would be like if this were all OK. (pause)

D) Now ask yourself: "If this were all resolved, at least for now, would there be anything else between me and feeling really good?" Let me know if something surfaces.

> *If anything else comes, then repeat (C) and (D) again and again, changing the phrasing to: "Now, if THESE were all resolved, etc. . . ." After the focuser has identified several things and put them aside, then change your phrasing of (D) to:*

Ask yourself, now: "Have I come to a space inside that would feel pretty good if these things I have set aside were resolved, or does something else still come up between me and feeling really good right now?" Let me know if you find anything.

> *Once the person has found such a space, continue with:*

E) Finally, take a few moments to find whether there are other things in your life now, *not* problems, which are important to you . . . maybe a challenge, a dream, something you are looking forward to . . . something it would be good to identify. If you find a couple of things like this, just note and put them aside like the rest. Say OK when you have done this.

2. *Feeling Which One is Number One*

> Now, return to whatever you have set aside and ask yourself: "Which one *feels* like it is Number One for me right now? For example, which one feels the heaviest, hurts the most, has the most energy, is most exciting?" Say OK when you have found it.

3. *Is It OK to Be with This?*

> Before going further, check for a moment to see
> if your body says it's OK to spend some time with
> this, giving it a more friendly hearing, allowing
> it to tell something of its story. Let me know if
> this is OK or not.
>
> > *If there is no difficulty, proceed to Step #4. If
> > there is significant difficulty or the answer is a
> > strong No, then ask:*
>
> All right, is it OK to be with how "difficult it feels
> to get into this right now?" ("scary," "overwhelm-
> ing," or whatever) (pause)
>
> > *If the answer to being with the difficulty is still
> > No, then go back to the inventory and find
> > something else that it is OK to be with.*

4. *Letting Go into It, Just Being in It, Sensing the Whole
   of It*

> Now, ask yourself: "How does this *whole* thing
> feel in my body right now? How am I carrying it
> inside me?" Allow your awareness to seep into
> your body, to settle in and sense how all this feels
> inside. Say OK when you can feel something of
> this in your body.
>
> > *If, when leading someone, you can tell that the
> > issue being worked with is something difficult,
> > then quietly suggest something like the follow-
> > ing:*
>
> Try to be with this whole thing in a more open,
> gentle, caring way. See if you can hold and feel it
> in the same way you might hold and feel a crying,

hurting child. Put your arm around it or hand on it if that helps. Perhaps put it next to you—whatever makes it easier for you to risk letting go into feeling how you carry this whole thing inside.

5. *Allowing It to Express Itself*

Now, staying with how this whole thing feels inside, see if anything comes, like a word or mental image, which expresses how it feels; anything that resonates or feels connected or on target inside. Take your time and let me know if something comes that fits the way this whole thing feels.

Recycling

If a symbol comes, continue the process as follows:

a) When a symbol is shared, let the person Focusing know that his or her symbol has been heard by reflecting it back to the focuser exactly as spoken. [If the person just nods or says, "OK," proceed to (b).] Then ask:

b) "Is this something that feels right to let unfold a little further?"

If the focuser says No, and wants to conclude his or her focusing, go to Step #6. If the focuser says Yes, and wants to continue, go to (c).

c) Ask yourself, "How does all this _____ (insert symbol if shared) now feel in my body? Take time to let go into and sense how all about this feels inside and let me know if anything comes that fits the way this now feels."

Remember to repeat the suggestion to be friendly with an issue whenever this might be helpful.

Once the Focusing process is moving along and it becomes clear the focuser can feel issues concretely in his or her body, it is no longer necessary to keep the directions for Steps #4 and #5 separate from one another. Instead, use these recycling steps.

Steps #4 and #5 are artificially separated in order to give the Focusing facilitator feedback as to whether or not the one Focusing (presumably a beginner) can allow himself or herself to feel anything connected with whatever is being focused on.

To summarize, then, the recycling process contains these steps:

1. Reflecting back, if appropriate (i.e., some symbol has been shared).

2. Checking to see if it feels right to go further.

3. Getting the felt sense of the new symbol.

4. Letting me (the facilitator) know if something else comes.

Continue with as many cycles as the focuser wants, or if you are pressed for time and you sense the person is in a better place you can ask:

"Check inside to see whether this feels like it should go further at this time, or if this is a place where it would feel right to stop, at least for now?"

If it is OK to stop, go to Step #6.

6. *Concluding Focusing with a Person*

A) Take a few moments, now, as you bring this period of quiet to an end, to become aware of any movement that may have taken place inside. First, recall how it felt in your body when you started to focus. (short pause) Now, come to where you are inside at present, sensing how this new place feels. Do you notice any difference? (pause)

> *Perhaps, you can draw the focuser out to share something of this very briefly while still staying with how it feels, eyes closed, etc., by asking:*
>
> *"Can you sense any easing or release in your body? Can you notice specifically any place where it feels less tight or tense?" (pause)*

B) Give yourself a little time, now, to get more familiar with this place where you decided to stop. Savor it. Notice how it feels so you can return later, if you wish. It is a stopping place for now, but can be a starting place at another time. (pause)

C) Finally, in whatever way seems right for you, give yourself a few more moments to be reverently in this place of gift within yourself; perhaps, to be in it prayerfully and gratefully before you stop. Then, whenever you're ready, you can stop.

What to do if someone can't get a felt sense (This is the person who knows a problem area with the mind but can't feel it in the body.)

1. Have this person ask himself or herself the following question, paying special attention to how their body responds:

    "I feel OK about this in my body, don't I?"

    Allow time for them to do this then ask: "Did you feel anything in your body that answered that? Just stay with this—be in it (Step #4). Let me know when you are familiar with this feeling."

2. Some people often have *a background feeling* that follows them around during the day. It is some way they always feel—always sad, always rushing, always trying hard. It often helps to touch and be with this background feeling.

3. Sometimes, it helps to pick two or three of the most important things the focuser has said if they have talked about what they are focusing on. Look for the most "feeling" statements. This may be a single word or phrase. Tell the person: "When I say what I'm going to say, don't you say anything to me or to yourself, just feel whatever comes."

Then slowly repeat the key words or phrases you have noted. Allow a little quiet time. Then, if they caught the edge of a felt sense, move through Focusing Steps #3, 4, and 5.

4. Ask how they feel about not being able to get hold of a felt sense.

5. Occasionally, it helps to stop focusing for a time and just allow the person to talk about his or her problem or concern. You respond with *healing listening*. If, while they are talking, you note a feeling tone coming into what they are saying, ask if they notice it. If so, see if that is something to focus on.

What to do if a felt sense doesn't express itself

1. If the person is working on a problem area, it sometimes helps to ask: "How does the worst of this feel in your body?"

   If what they are working on is a happy, exciting thing, ask: "How does the best of this feel in your body?"

2. Sometimes it helps to ask forward-moving or positive questions:
      "What would feel like a small step forward with all this?"
      "What needs to happen in your body for this to be OK?"
      "What would feel like a breath of fresh air in this whole thing?"

3. Often, it helps to make a friendly space next to a felt sense that refuses to shift. Gently check into

this place a few times a day to see if anything new has come. Don't avoid this place, but don't be there all the time either. Just make a friendly place to come and wait.

4. Sometimes you can try the following with a painful felt sense:

    "Imagine, for a moment, how it would feel inside if this whole thing were just the opposite of what it is now and everything were OK." (After a pause) "Can you feel this way all the time?" (If the answer is "No," say:) Ask yourself: "What needs to change inside me for this to feel better?"

    If something comes, see if this new body clue provides any direction to follow with the painful felt sense.

5. If none of the above seem to help and the focuser remains stuck with a felt sense that won't unfold, try the following. Ask the person if it feels right for a few moments to put their felt sense on the back burner and just talk a bit about what they are focusing on or the difficulty they may be having. Then just listen with healing listening. If feelings surface in the person during such listening, see if one or other of these might provide a slightly different doorway into the felt sense.

Six suggestions
for facilitators

1.   The facilitator's role is: a) to guide a focuser through the steps, and b) to create a trusting, caring, more secure climate within which it is easier to risk Focusing. The facilitator creates this environment by the quality of presence in the relationship, one which flows out of personal maturity and caring detachment. Such an atmosphere encourages and disposes for Focusing, and is, in itself, a gift that heals and opens for further grace.

2.   Remember, the nature of your response as a facilitator is not to make cognitive connections of insight but to support a forward movement of felt meaning within the one Focusing. This means your interventions should be intended to help an organismic process unfold. You're not there to talk *about* an issue, but to help the person remain in their bodily felt carrying of that issue so it can tell its story.

3.   Be ready to skip Steps #1 and #2 if the issue to be focused on is clearly evident. For example, something upsetting has just happened. *Always* check, though, to determine whether it is OK to be with this particular issue (Step #3), then go on through Steps #4 to #6.

4.   Remember, the focuser cannot focus while you, the facilitator, are talking or giving directions. Be brief and clear. Say what you have to say in order to support the process, then get out of the way and be quiet so the one Focusing can continue.

5.   Always give clear ground rules so those Focusing know what to do next, and how they are to let you

know when they have done what you have asked. This frees the focuser to concentrate on Focusing and you from worrying about whether it's evident how you are to be called upon if further assistance is needed.

6.   If at any point you become unsure about what to do next, ask the one focusing: "What does it feel right to do now?" If the answer is: "I don't know," then ask whether it would be OK just to sit with that feeling of unsureness for a bit and see whether anything comes from that.

The interface between science and religion

A believing born of change

Whatever the limitations of religion might be, it seems destined in some fashion to assist at the birth of a new consciousness. But the religious quest is invariably a two-edged sword. While one believer may narrow religion to gratify some obsessive need for ultimate security, another will deepen through maturing presence into the transcendent awareness of greater Mystery.

When considering religion's support for human transformation, *what* is believed seems somehow less important than the act of *believing* itself. It is the *process* more than the *content* of faith that seems to shed light on the evolution of human wholeness. Gordon Allport found that:

> . . . the precise ecclesiastical position of the individual is not an index of the maturity of his religious sentiment. Adherence to almost any church, or to none at all, may mark those who in their maturing personalities have fought through the issues of religion.[1]

Abraham Maslow arrived at a similar conclusion:

> . . . a "serious" Buddhist, let us say, one who is con-
> cerned with "ultimate concerns" and with Tillich's
> "dimension of depth," is more co-religionist to a "se-
> rious" agnostic than he is to a conventional, super-
> ficial, other-directed Buddhist for whom religion is
> only habit or custom, i.e., "behavior."[2]

Citizenship in the Mystery seems to rest on something beyond a shared content of belief. There is a more
durable believing that is not based upon dogma or ideas
but upon *changing perspective*. We are reminded of those
poignant words which Tennyson put upon the lips of a
dying king:

> And slowly answer'd Arthur from the barge:
> "The old order changeth, yielding place to new,
> And God fulfills himself in many ways. . . ."[3]

What, precisely, establishes *an old order?* Is it not
the way things are seen? And must an old order not inevitably be transformed as people gain a new perception of
themselves?

The question now, as we formulate it, is whether or
not God is fulfilled precisely *because* the old order
changes? Is there a higher continuity in the on-going *transition* from one order to the next? Is there an invitation
which sounds at the core of our being, perpetually sum-
moning us beyond the limited perspective of each passing
moment? Are faith and vision somehow nurtured within
the crucible of change itself? Is *believing* actually an
awareness and living out of this changing perspective?

There are several ways to explore this intriguing possibility. We will consider two approaches. One, surpris-
ingly, is found within the field of modern theoretical physics. The other, from theology, has its origin in an ancient
biblical viewpoint. Both approaches deal directly with the

issue of consciousness evolution. They both regard changing perspective as integral to human development. Both show a remarkable degree of convergence in their methodology and conclusions. They focus the lens of scientific investigation upon what we have referred to as "the Body of Spirit." The convergence is so striking that we may have here the beginning of that longed-for rapprochement between science and religion which Teilhard de Chardin so ardently sought.

Let's start with a recent development that has excited speculation far beyond the field of its immediate practical application. Holography is a type of photography in which a laser beam is split with a half-silvered mirror in order to illuminate both the subject being photographed and the photographic plate itself. The pattern actually recorded on film, the hologram, does not resemble the original scene in any way. However, when a laser beam of the same wavelength as that initially used is passed through the developed holographic transparency, a viewer on the other side sees a three-dimensional image of what was originally recorded.

The intriguing aspect of a hologram, though, is how it stores information. It does this in a fashion totally unlike conventional photography. This is what excites its proponents and has led to applications of holographic theory far beyond the realm of optical imagery in film and television.

If a small piece is broken or cut from the holographic plate and the same wavelength of laser light is directed toward this divided portion, *the entire original scene can still be seen through this smaller segment of the transparency*. This happens because information about the total scene is present within every part of the hologram. *The whole is contained in each part of the holographic image*.

All of the whole is within every part! We've touched on this before in our discussion of *soma* (body). Now, however, we're finding the same phenomenon appearing in modern theoretical physics.

Neuroscientists are already applying holographic theory to the human brain where there is still no adequate explanation of memory retention. Surgery indicates that even though a considerable portion of the brain is removed, memory still remains. So now, instead of seeking an isolated site or location for remembering, some researchers hypothesize that memory may be distributed throughout the entire brain, especially in the cortical layers. It is as though *all* of the memory is stored *in every part* of the cortex, much as the entire holographic image is stored in every segment of the plate that receives it.

But how does this recent development contribute to a fuller appreciation of a believing that is born of change? How can an understanding of the hologram enrich our perspective on what it means to believe?

Mystics, philosophers, and sages from every age and culture hold that there is an underlying unity behind the apparent multiplicity which ordinary people experience. Metaphysics has stressed the fundamental oneness of being which lies beneath the diversity that strikes our senses. Some thinkers have even gone so far as to say that our everyday perception that sees the world in terms of separation, distinctness, and temporal succession is fundamentally an illusion. Unity is reality for these persons, and everything else is considered a deceitful mirage which clouds the senses and distracts us from the main issues of human existence. In the name of an all-encompassing unity they scornfully reject the reality of multiplicity and even history itself, dismissing sensory data as basically untrue.

We strongly disagree with this view because of our deep conviction that history and *Chronos* are not an illusion. Despite all arguments to the contrary, people do have a past, a present, and some sort of future. Survival depends upon interaction between a knowing subject and an external world. *There is an interface between the organism and its environment.* There is temporal spread-outness in *sarx* (the flesh) which generates history, multiplicity, and movement. And yet, despite what we consider excesses in the views of some mystical authors, there remains a certain truth in their position once it can be placed within a more balanced setting.

But granting both unity *and* multiplicity, what does all this and holograms have to do with believing? One more bit of data and the pieces will begin to fall into place.

Classical physics used to view the world as an interaction of separate, distinct particles. A pluralistic, dichotomized universe of multiplicity. Physicist David Bohm calls this experienced separateness *the explicate order*. It is a perspective within which the scientist as observer is clearly distinct from the object observed.

However, this view does not explain certain anomalies which occur in certain experiments where the usual common sense view of reality seems to break down. Sometimes, for example, a particle will appear to be present simultaneously in every part of the system being measured. The notion of autonomous separateness and more traditional causal interaction does not adequately explain what happens throughout the course of this apparently contradictory event. During certain experiments things do not appear as distinct and separable as we would like them to be. One notices a blurring of the expected division between observing subject and observed object, as well as between objects that interact outside the observer. It's all rather like Maslow's experience with the taste of strawberries in his daughter's mouth.

Experiments like this shake the very foundations of our ordinary perceptions of reality. They imply a unity which our prejudiced senses find it difficult to accept. David Bohm suggests a solution

> . . . by postulating that the structure of the universe is holographic, with its entire explicate structure encoded in its every part. Since the whole of the universe is enfolded in every subregion, Bohm claims that there exists a further order. In addition to the

explicate order, the order of multiplicity, there exists the *implicate order,* the order of undivided wholeness.

"Every kind of 'particle' which in current physics is said to be a basic constituent of matter will have to be discussed . . . (in such a way that) . . . 'particles' are no longer considered as autonomous and separately existent. Thus, we come to a new general physical description in which 'everything implicates everything' in an order of undivided wholeness."[4]

By postulating a holographic structure for the universe itself, Bohm goes a long way toward resolving tension between the world of multiplicity and the world of unity with which mystics have always struggled. Instead of damning one side of the equation and relegating it to the realm of illusion, Bohm leaves open the happy possibility that both experiences are valid and interact with one another in a consistent, constructive fashion.

At this point, however, the plot thickens. Having established both experimentally and theoretically that quantum mechanics points toward the existence of an implicate order, Bohm then goes on to consider the actual unfolding itself, that inner *movement* from implicate to explicate which grounds an appearance of "the whole" within each part. This fundamental *movement,* we feel, is what surfaces in the Focusing process. The human organism knows its connectedness. That connectedness appears within and *as* the unfolding of each felt sense. The body's knowing of holographic tied-in-ness is expressed within the forward *movement* of felt meaning. Focusing allows this embodied sense for deeper unification to surface within the very process which carries it forward.

David Bohm has not been content to rest with a wellworn mystical expression of underlying unity. He has pressed on toward a more basic issue—the actual process which grounds *both* implicate and explicate orders.

In a fascinating interview published in the *Journal of Transpersonal Psychology,* Bohm expands on this theme in response to questions from John Welwood.

> *Bohm:* The energy which moves between the explicate and implicate orders is still further inward. It is the force which brings about the unfolding of the implicate. You see, we have the explicate order and the implicate order, and the movement from one to the other—which is the holomovement.

> *Welwood:* So in your framework the holomovement is the movement between the implicate and the explicate?

> *Bohm:* Right. The holomovement is more "inward" than the two orders which are its extremes. And beyond all this is that emptiness and fullness which is entirely implicit, which cannot be uttered.

> *Welwood: Entirely implicit.* you're making a distinction between the implicate order and something beyond it, which is entirely implicit.

> *Bohm:* That's right. "Implicate" still means that something could be said about it. But the ultimate ground of being is entirely unutterable, entirely implicit.

> *Welwood:* Would you agree that both our thought and our intuition are permeated by that unutterable? Even when we are confused?

> *Bohm:* Yes, in some sense. We could say everything exists in that.

> . . . In the holomovement one end is the implicate, the other the explicate. The movement between is more fundamental. So the holomovement is not an *interaction* between implicate and explicate orders; rather it is the ground of both.[5]

The holomovement is the ground of both! And beyond all this lies an emptiness and *fullness* which cannot be uttered. Is this a physicist's way of approaching the mystic experience of God?

Be that as it may, we quote this fascinating bit of dialogue because it raises the question we want to examine. *Is believing actually the maturing awareness which each person has of this unutterable ground of being, the holomovement and whatever lies beyond?* Is it some gifted experience which can arise from the heart of each Focusing process?

Rather than measuring faith by some content that is believed, ought we not, instead, to be looking toward that bodily awareness which in some dim fashion already grasps our tied-in-ness to an evolving Body of Spirit? Bohm identifies an underlying process—the holomovement. We ask whether there might not be a special kind of consciousness that can perceive this movement, and we are suggesting that such a perspective and perception is what has been traditionally meant by *"believing."*

Faith is always viewed as somehow different from reason. Perhaps reason can be situated developmentally as a knowing associated with survival in the flesh (*sarx*). Reason aims toward control. It is a magnificent tool for problem-solving which thrives on calculation and logic, attention to detail, understanding the laws of nature, technical know-how, repeatability, and predictability in experimentation. It is the basic stuff of scientific method.

Faith, on the other hand, comes to grips with a more profound kind of existence. It includes awareness in which goals stretch far beyond the maintenance of individual biological integrity. Believing looks beyond survival to *evolution*. It is a consciousness drawn toward the unfolding of *Pneuma* (Spirit). It is an awareness of and living of the very *movement* which carries an individual and the species forward.

This calls for a basic attitude not of control but of *allowing*. One takes a different stance before the Unutterable. *Believing* differs from reasoning not only because *religious* things are thought about, but because the way in which one perceives is radically different.

Focusing encourages this evolutionary change in perspective. There is a special kind of knowing in *kairos*. The feeling is one of allowing, letting go, dropping the reins. This is not *doing* but *being drawn forward.* Believing, we feel, is an embodied, felt awareness of living within such movement as it gradually reveals the Larger Whole.

David Bohm has pointed his finger toward a very precise energy at work in consciousness evolution. That energy is not some observable *content* in either the explicate or implicate orders. Rather, it is a broader process which grounds the two before fading off beyond all present human knowing into some unutterable fullness.

Focusing is a very practical way of allowing ourselves to be drawn forward one step at a time on the long journey into this holomovement. It is a doorway beyond reason into faith. Not faith in the sense of specific doctrines of belief, but a believing that is the gift and expression of some deeper awareness. It is letting go into the very flow of evolution that brings us home to a Greater Self-Process.

Bohm, like Gendlin, directs attention toward this underlying movement. Let's turn, now, to the biblical viewpoint. How is such a developmental perspective expressed in the language of theology?

The revelation of human metamorphosis can be discovered in the writings of St. Paul. It is contained in a fascinating Greek term—*anakephalaiosis*. This strange word is really about *self* and, more precisely, about the cosmic dimension of Self-Process.

> For he has made known to us in all wisdom and insight the mystery of his will, according to his purpose which he set forth in Christ as a plan for the fullness (*pleroma*) of time (*kairos*), to unite (*anakephalaiosis*) all things in him, things in heaven and things on earth. (*Eph. 1:9-10 RSV*)

Anakephalaiosis is a developmental word describing a vast process of unification. The corresponding term coined by Teilhard de Chardin was *Christogenesis*. Christ, for him, was a process. Cosmic evolution (*cosmogenesis*) moved forward within the framework of this still greater Mystery. In fact, cosmogenesis for Teilhard was Christogenesis.

The key to this blending of evolution with Christian faith lay in Teilhard's growing realization that the appearance or *epiphany* of God in Jesus Christ was only the prelude to an even more dramatic and cosmic appearance of the divine. The birth of Jesus was a first step in an immense process that would culminate one day for Christian believers in a unified sense of "I" spoken by the Cosmic Christ.

But if epiphany is the beginning, then divine *diaphany* is the process which follows. This word, also coined by Teilhard, describes a growing *transparency* of the cosmos. In his view, realization of rootedness in some deeper Movement breaks through within the humanity of a unique individual, the God-Man, Jesus of Nazareth. But following this beginning, that same realization is meant to continue to appear along a broad *front* of evolution. This is what Teilhard means by *the Divine Milieu*. For Christians, the potential for cosmic congruence locked within the humanity of every person is in some way ineradicably touched by a realization which broke through in the carpenter from Galilee.

In an earlier work *Becoming a Person in the Whole Christ*,[6] we described *diaphany* in language that a photographer might use to illustrate this phenomenon. When one is engaged in darkroom portrait printing, he or she lays a sheet of photographic paper under the enlarger and briefly exposes a negative image of the subject for several seconds. After exposure, the paper remains as blank as it was in the beginning. There is no image. But then the paper is dipped in a chemical bath. At first, nothing happens. But soon, almost miraculously, the outline of a face begins to appear. Slowly, at first, the very dark portions appear followed by the subtle and softer highlights. Gradually, eyes, cheeks, the gentle play of light on hair, and background images—all begin to emerge. Diaphany is something like this. Within the framework of Christian thought it is a dawning of God which breaks through along an entire *front* of evolution. The divine hologram emerges in all its striking totality. "It is no longer I who live, but Christ who lives in me. . ." (*Gal. 2:20 RSV*)

Anakephalaiosis, for Christians, is the developing awareness which cosmogenesis has of itself! It is the maturing of a bodily-felt congruence that breaks forth like dawn on the mountaintops to catch up individual centers of consciousness in an even greater flow of meaning, experience, and purpose. A single unified *soma* (body) unfolds. The individual human lives poured forth to grace this planet with awareness become, each in their turn, a living cell, an emerging felt sense, the quivering personal edge of this vast unfolding awareness.

The Greek word *kephale* literally means *head*. The prefix *ana-* signifies *movement into*. Christ is spoken of as *head* in the sense that he is both the source of this expanding consciousness as well as the governing and unifying principle of his Body which is cosmic in scope. In much the same fashion, the entire hologram is both source and unifying principle of its expression within each single part.

But the Christology of *anakephalaiosis* is fundamentally a Christology of *development,* forward movement into (*ana-*). As the German theologian, Karl Rahner, notes:

> In its real and essential being Christianity really understands itself as an existential process, and this process is precisely what we are calling a personal relationship to Jesus Christ.[7]

The Process is the Message, the Message is the Process.

Anakephalaiosis is a way in which biblical theology recognizes the deeper embodied movement which grounds what David Bohm has spoken of as the implicate and explicate orders. In a holographic sense, each person mirrors within his or her own self-process that larger flow of consciousness and meaning which both includes and transcends every individual particle. The total hologram transcends each part and is yet being repeated in all its entirety within those same parts. This sense of *unfolding togetherness* is as difficult for us to describe as it was for the Apostle Paul. Anglican Bishop John A.T. Robinson notes how

> Paul clearly feels the painful inadequacy of language to convey the unique "withness" that Christians have in Christ. It is surely clear that for Paul to do or suffer anything "with" Christ speaks of no external concomitance, like the P.T. instructor who says, "Now do this with me," but of a common organic functioning, as the new tissues take on the rhythms and metabolism of the body into which they have been grafted.[8]

There is an edge of Mystery, then, that develops as people grow. They catch quick glimpses out of the corners of their eyes. They have a tangible sense, now and then, of life stirring just ahead of, around, and within their unfolding awareness. A new rhythm and a new metabolism emerge. Words generally fail when trying to express what is there.

Most people tend to project this greater reality *outside of* themselves. Some people, however, eventually re-own the experience. This seems to be what healthy religion is all about. For a fleeting instant a person turns the universe inside-out, catching sight of the Mystery unfolding within their own personal becoming. The response is generally gratitude mixed with a curious, exhilarating sense of self-possession in which there can be an extraordinary kind of congruence. This is fertile, sacred ground where the seeds of worship strike deep root and one is simultaneously great and yet oh so small!

Anakephalaiosis is a theological word that corresponds in some fashion with what David Bohm has described as the holomovement. It is the more readily accessible process which bonds both implicate and explicate orders, unveiling the vision of a greater *Soma* (Body). Believing is the emerging consciousness which this Larger Body has of itself. The dawn of Spirit Awareness.

But the Mystery, for Bohm, is by no means ended with the holomovement. Beyond all this there yet remains "that emptiness and fullness which is entirely implicit, which cannot be uttered." For Christians, too, there is the revelation of yet another dimension to this incredible drama.

> ... and when all things are thus subject to him [*Christ*], then the Son himself will also be made subordinate to God [*The Father*] who made all things subject to him, and thus God will be all in all. (*1 Cor. 15:28 NEB*)

We come, finally, to that supreme Mystery of Christian revelation—*the Sacred Trinity!* There remains an even more profound process of unification which includes, yet stretches light years beyond, the Christ in whom individual believers are incorporated. Trinitarian life lies at the heart of *God as Process.* Here is the focal point of Christian belief and a potential revelation that may be capable of unlocking the very secret of consciousness itself. The Christian God is process, and the unfolding of God through Christ and in *Pneuma* (the Spirit) tends toward a point of fullness in *Kairos* when "God will be all in all."

Once again, an arcane Greek word, *perichoresis*, lies at the heart of Trinitarian theology. The word means *pen-*

etration, and in more precise language it indicates the necessary *being-in-one-another* of the three divine persons in the Trinity. This term preserves the distinctness of persons while at the same time it describes the underlying unity that results, finally, in there being only *one* God. The Father begets the Son, and the mutual dialogue of love between Father and Son results in *Pneuma* (the Spirit). *Perichoresis* is literally *a divine dance,* an eternal holomovement or flow among distinct persons in the unity of a single Godhead. The Father is totally in the Son, the Son is totally in the Father. The Spirit is totally in both Son and Father and equally penetrated by them in return.

Perichoresis, for the average person, is perhaps best found within the experience of shared love; it is most vividly realized when the love is equally given and received. It surfaces in those non-manipulative moments of closeness and intimacy when people can simply rest in and enjoy one another's presence. It involves a *being with* that is always more than the physical proximity of bodies. It's like enjoying one's children as they play and wanting to gobble them up because they are so loveable in their antics. It's like being with a very close friend who knows you better than you know yourself and with whom you find the freedom and courage to be. The union of spouses, the quick glance of mutual understanding and remembrance—all these are holographic flashes of *perichoresis,* the stuff of being distinct and yet simultaneously *having our being in one another.* One finds here a maturing sense of mutuality and presence which begins to transcend the physical division between separated bodies. It is an experience not only of being *with* but being *within* one another which dimly reflects through our limited perceptual capability that "unutterable" cosmic *perichoresis* which bonds the universe and the very inner life of God.

This experience of having-one's-being-within or being-in one-another is a cardinal principle both in New Testament revelation and in Christian theology. Jesus goes to great lengths, usually with mixed results, to teach this mystery to his puzzled disciples.

Thomas said to him, "Lord, we do not know where
you are going; how can we know the way?" Jesus said
to him, "I am the way, and the truth, and the life; no
one comes to the Father, but by me. If you had known
me, you would have known my Father also; hence-
forth you know him and have seen him." Philip said
to him, "Lord, show us the Father, and we shall be
satisfied." Jesus said to him, "Have I been with you
so long, and yet you do not know me, Philip? He who
has seen me has seen the Father; how can you say,
"Show us the Father?" Do you not believe that I am
in the Father and the Father in me? The words that
I say to you I do not speak on my own authority; but
the Father who dwells in me does his works. Believe
me that I am in the Father and the Father in me. . . .
(*John 14:5-11 RSV*)

In its own way, like theoretical physics, Christian
theology has had to find a way beyond the perception of
reality which divides everything into separable particles.
Philosophers and theologians have always struggled with
the problem of unity in diversity, the perennial problem
of the one and the many. There has been an almost in-
tuitive recognition that while the multiplicity associated
with sensory data is important, it still cannot of itself provide a sufficiently comprehensive basis upon which to
build an adequate metaphysics and theology. The degree
of sophistication which eventually evolved in Christian
theology is truly remarkable because it emerged in an age
when the perception of evolution and process was almost
non-existent.

It is important to realize that although the early theologians lived in an age that was dominated by quantity
and particle perception, they still managed to develop a
theology capable in its own way of transcending the re
stricted categories and thought patterns associated with
this limited view of reality. The notion of *perichoresis* goes
totally against ordinary sense perception. Three persons,
even though divine, cannot simultaneously be distinct
and yet be one!

The perceptual capability, which was slow to evolve and which now promises to revolutionize the entire expression of Christian theology, was *a sense for development,* evolution, and, most important, *self-process.* As long as the category of quantity or content was dominant, the growth of theology was hamstrung by the restricted perceptual framework associated with that limited view.

Now, however, it is becoming evident that the experiential ground for an awareness of unity in differentiation is to be found in the transcendent experience associated with self-process. Focusing allows this unity to become manifest *within the bodily felt experience of development itself* and especially within the unfolding sense of "I."

The paradox of unity in multiplicity is resolved within an experience of holomovement without destroying either side of the equation! What needs to be better understood, however, is the nature of the process itself. This is where physics, psychology, and theology now share exciting common ground. *Perichoresis,* which indicates an unfolding within the Godhead (a divine Self-Process), together with the awareness found in successful Focusing could well be the links that bond these disparate disciplines into a rich possibility for unification. A truly formidable next step for humankind may be taking shape. The convergence of science and religion is fast approaching.

Each person, according to the Judaeo-Christian tradition, is created *in the image and likeness of God.* Our own consciousness, therefore, according to this most ancient revelation, is modeled upon the "unutterable" fullness of God. Father, Son, and Spirit are theological points of differentiation within the eternal *perichoresis.* Yet each one, simultaneously, may represent the more ultimate ground of that unique differentiation that animates the Christian believer's self-process.

Examine the movement yourself. *"I"* focus on *"a felt*

sense" and the felt sense *"unfolds"* into who I am in the process of becoming. One may reasonably apply a Trinitarian model to that very flow of awareness through which consciousness evolves.

A threefold differentiation appears during Focusing. It may seem an oversimplification to suggest that these three elements are related holographically to the inner life of God. Yet the similarity, as revealed within the Judaeo-Christian tradition, is too striking to ignore. It presents, after all, a tantalizing possibility. The very process of consciousness which Focusing unveils in each one of us is but the holographic expression of that greater consciousness in whose image we all are fashioned.

The idea is not altogether new. Our intention here has been to suggest a remarkable link between the dynamics of Focusing and a Trinitarian perspective on the inner life of God. But the notion that consciousness may extend holographically within Bohm's hypothesis of an implicate order has already been proposed. In his article titled "A Holographic Model of Transpersonal Consciousness" Robert M. Anderson, Jr., suggested the following:

> . . . since the universe is holographically complex, the universe may be conscious on the implicate level. It would then be conscious to a far higher degree than any human being is on the level of personal consciousness. The universe at the implicate level is almost infinitely more complex than the brain; it enfolds the explicate order throughout its structure.
>
> When a person . . . comes into touch with consciousness at the implicate level, a consciousness he always has subliminally but of which he is not usually immediately aware, it is not *he* that experiences the cosmic consciousness. . . . When transpersonal consciousness is experienced, the individual self "falls away" as personal consciousness resonates to and merges with the universe and the implicate order.[9]

Once again, an echo of St. Paul: ". . . it is no longer I who live, but Christ who lives in me. . . ." (*Gal. 2:20 RSV*)

Anderson paints in broad strokes without addressing some of the finer *developmental* points which we believe a Trinitarian perspective may add to our understanding of how consciousness evolves. A Trinitarian viewpoint introduces the element of *differentiation* which allows for development and process. Such inner diversity affects the very structure of consciousness itself within the Christian view of God.

A pantheistic finale would have us all absorbed into some amorphous lump. *Unity at the expense of differentiation!* This is exactly the opposite of a Trinitarian viewpoint. *Unity in differentiation!* The holomovement (*perichoresis*) functions within the framework of a dynamic interplay between individuality *and* growing unification. It extends the image of God into a likeness repeated over and over again within the unfolding of each individual center of human awareness.

When Focusing on a felt sense, one is never completely *outside* of that upon which one focuses. The felt sense is not altogether object. Yet neither is it completely one's self. There is a differentiation, an interface, an abyss. One has not yet *come home*.

But when the felt sense *unfolds,* when this initially inarticulate word becomes flesh, there is that forward rushing movement which tells us who we are. The story moves on. There is something of Father, Son, and Spirit in each of us. Christians view themselves as created in the image of this inner life of God, that unutterable source from whom all life and consciousness ultimately flow.

Perhaps the theology of Holy Spirit (the Third Person of the Trinity—*Pneuma*) has been slow to develop within Christianity precisely because the sense for self-process and development is still so little appreciated. But Spirit *is* the holographic process, the movement, the unfolding, the *felt shift* which unites Father and Son, human and divine, head and members, focuser and felt sense.

There is an ancient Christian prayer, centuries old yet filled with a richness of realization, that is only now, perhaps, ripening to the fullness of its potential.

Emitte Spiritum Tuum et creabuntur, et renovabis faciem terrae.

Send forth Thy Spirit and they shall be created, and Thou shalt renew the face of the earth.

Unity, peace, brotherhood, the diminishment of destructive human aggressions—these are tangible milestones marking progress along the journey into ourselves which *is* the journey into God. But belief in God, as such, does not and never has addressed the critical issues of war and peace, love, unity, and the unfolding of self-esteem. History bears tragic and repeated witness to the savage destruction of human life and property that has occurred in the name of belief in all manner of gods. On the other hand, human beings who believe in themselves and come to value themselves deeply neither destroy one another nor the world around them.

The difficulty with so much in religion is that *it remains outside the felt sense and self-process of the individual believer.* So many symbols, revelations, traditions, and teachings fill the content of belief without nourishing the process of believing. A plague of violence continues to scourge the face of our planet, and religion often becomes its unwitting tool when attention is focused too narrowly on the formal content of belief.

Perhaps the real power of religious symbols remains largely unrealized because the potential for believing associated with *any* effective symbol is not yet fully appreciated. Whenever ordinary symbols move meaning forward, they inevitably extend the transcending process which is the unfolding of deeper Mystery. The flow of felt meaning, any meaning, *is already an innately religious event.* Perhaps the best symbol for God, therefore, *is the experience of unfolding itself.* And if one must still name such an event, let the naming dawn in a realization that "I Am Who I Am" (*Exod. 3:14 RSV*) is more than Yahweh's response to the prophet. It is the holographic Mystery of an unfolding sense of Self. The Whole is in the part, and the part is in the Whole, and "I Am Who I Am" is the edge of awareness, the believing born of change that announces the *Pleroma*, the *Kairos*, the advancing "fullness of him who fills all in all." (*Eph. 1:23 RSV*)

Learnings we value
in searching for
a bio-spirituality

1. Learning to *let go of the controlling mind* and its ef
    fort to manipulate everything. The best way to "get
    out of the mind" is to get into the body.

2. Learning to allow your own unique life-meaning and
    direction to emerge from a process *felt right within
    the organism*.

3. Learning to *trust* this meaning as it gradually un-
    folds.

4. Learning the *language of bodily knowing* as it leads
    toward a sense for greater wholeness and connect-
    edness.

5. Finding a doorway into the Body of Spirit *within the
    unfolding edge* of your own personal life story. The
    Message is the Process, and the Process is the Mes-
    sage.

6.   Learning to sense the inside awareness of personal unfolding *as the core* of your own *believing*.

7.   Allowing yourself to be *available for surprise*. Growing to welcome it as a gift and a friend.

8.   Learning to identify your own *resistances* to Focusing as challenging *doorways to further growth*. This experience nourishes the roots of hope—there is never any life-circumstance within which you cannot find some pathway to change.

9.   Learning to give negative feelings a gentle, friendly hearing. Allowing what scares or confuses you an opportunity to tell its story. Imagery can help in this process—i.e., the example of holding a crying, hurting child as a way of being with negative, difficult feelings.

Notes

Preface

1. Carl G. Jung, *Psychology and Religion: West and East,* Collected Works, Vol. II (New York: Pantheon, 1958) p. 537.

Introduction

1. Pierre Teilhard De Chardin, *The Future of Man*, Translated from the French by Norman Denny (New York: Harper & Row, 1964) p. 90.

2. Eugene T. Gendlin, Ph.D., *Focusing*, Second edition, New, revised instructions (New York: Bantam Books, 1981).

3. Pierre Teilhard De Chardin, *The Phenomenon of Man*(New York: Harper & Brothers Publishers, 1959) pp. 284-285.

4. Abraham H. Maslow, *Religions, Values, and Peak Experiences* (Columbus: Ohio State University Press, 1964) pp.11, xiv, xiii.

Chapter 2

1. Eugene T. Gendlin, Ph.D., *Focusing, op.cit.*
2. *Ibid.*, p. 77.

Chapter 4

1. Pierre Teilhard de Chardin, *The Phenomenon of Man, op.cit.*, p. 311.
2. Michael Murphy, *Jacob Atabet—A Speculative Fiction* (Millbrae, California: Celestial Arts, 1977).

Chapter 5

1. Alan Watts, *The Book—On the Taboo Against Knowing Who You Are* (New York: Pantheon Books, 1966) p. 11.

Chapter 6

1. Eugene T. Gendlin, Ph.D., *Focusing, op.cit.*, p. 77.

Chapter 7

1. Pierre Teilhard de Chardin, *The Future of Man, op.cit.*, p. 280.
2. William James, *The Varieties of Religious Experience* (New York: The New American Library, A Mentor Book, 1958) p. 388.
3. Dom Sebastian Moore, *God Is a New Language* (Westminster, Maryland: The Newman Press, 1967) p. 54.

4. Karl Rahner, "Christology and an Evolutionary World View," in *Theology Digest,* Vol. 28, No. 3, Fall 1980, p. 2ll.

5. Sir Arthur Eddington as quoted by David Foster in *The Intelligent Universe—A Cybernetic Philosophy* (New York: G.P. Putnam's Sons, 1975) pp. 164-65. Mr. Foster is quoting from Sir Arthur Eddington's remarks in *The Nature of the Physical World* (London: J. M. Dent and Sons Ltd.) 1935.

Chapter 8

1. Carl G. Jung, *Modern Man in Search of a Soul,* translated by W. S. Dell and Cary F. Baynes (New York: Harcourt, Brace & World, Inc., A Harvest Book, 1963; first published in 1933) p. 235.

2. *Ibid.,* p. 219-220.

3. Carl G. Jung, *Psychology and Religion: West and East, op.cit.,* p. 535-537.

4. Gregory Baum, *Man Becoming; God in Secular Experience* (New York: Herder & Herder, 1970) p. 2G4.

5. Abraham Maslow, *Religions, Values, and Peak Experiences, op.cit.,* p. xiv.

Appendix 2

1. Gordon W. Allport, *The Individual and His Religion* (New York: The Macmillan Company, Macmillan Paperbacks Edition, 1960) p. 68.

2. Abraham H. Maslow, *Religions, Values, and Peak Experiences, op.cit.,* p. 56.

3. Alfred Tennyson, "The Passing of Arthur," in *The Poetical Works of Tennyson,* with new Introduction by G. Robert Strange (Boston: Cambridge Editions, Houghton Mifflin Co., 1974) p. 449.

4. Robert M. Anderson, Jr., "A Holographic Model of Transpersonal Consciousness," in *The Journal of Transpersonal Psychology,* Vol. 9, No. 2, 1977, p. 123. The quotation comes from David Bohm, "Quantum theory as an indication of a new order in physics. Part B. Implicate and explicate order in physical law." *Foundations of Physics,* 1973,3,2, 139-68.

5. David Bohm, John Welwood, "Issues in Physics, Psychology and Metaphysics: A Conversation," in *The Journal of Transpersonal Psychology,* Vol. 12, No. 1, 1980, pp. 26-28 *passim.*

6. Edwin M. McMahon and Peter A. Campbell, *Becoming a Person in the Whole Christ* (New York: Sheed & Ward, 1967).

7. Karl Rahner, *Foundations of Christian Faith—An Introduction to the Idea of Christianity,* translated by William V. Dych (New York: The Seabury Press, A Crossroad Book, 1978) p. 306.

8. John A. T. Robinson, *The Body—A Study in Pauline Theology* (London: SCM Press Ltd., 1963) p. 63.

9. Robert M. Anderson, Jr., "A Holographic Model of Transpersonal Consciousness," *op.cit.,* pp. 126-127.

The Institute for Research in Spirituality

In 1976 a group of Christians from all walks of life came together to explore ways in which research and experience in the human sciences could better be integrated with the Christian tradition. Together, these people formed a non-profit organization to support research that would:

1) Clarify what is psychologically healthy in religion and religious practice as well as what contributes to pathology in religion

2) Integrate a Christian theology that contributes to human wholeness with sound psychological growth processes

3) Design practical programs for spiritual growth

4) Establish a network of centers through which these programs would be available to the public

5) Support the publication of materials contribution to healthy Christial spirituality

Information about the current schedule of workshops on Focusing and Spirituality conducted by Rev. Edwin M. McMahon, Ph.D., and Rev. Peter A. Campbell, Ph.D., as well as a list of other Institute literature on Focusing and Spirituality is available by writing:

The Institute for Research in Spirituality
6305 Greely Hill Road
Coulterville, CA 95311